proustian space

proustian space

By

GEORGES POULET

Translated by ELLIOTT COLEMAN

THE JOHNS HOPKINS UNIVERSITY PRESS

Baltimore and London

The Johns Hopkins University Press, Baltimore, Maryland 21218
The Johns Hopkins Press Ltd., London

Library of Congress Catalog Card Number 76-47390
ISBN 0-8018-1921-0

Library of Congress Cataloging in Publication data will be found on
the last printed page of this book.

Translator's Note

The translator is most grateful to the author
for his kind assistance with this translation.

E. C.

preface

"WE JUXTAPOSE," says Bergson, "our states of consciousness in such a way as to perceive them simultaneously:
not one following the other, but one alongside the other;
in brief, we project time into space."

This is perhaps the most serious piece of criticism address-
ed by Bergsonism to the intellect. Intellect would tend to
annihilate the true continuity of our being, by substituting
for it a sort of mental space in which the moments would
align themselves without ever interpenetrating themselves.
Hence, there is for Bergson the necessity of destroying this
"space" in order to come back by intuition to pure duration, to the modulated murmur by which existence reveals
its inexhaustibly changing nature to the mind. It is singular
that one who had so often been taken for a disciple of
Bergson should have assumed, probably without knowing
it, a position diametrically opposite. If the thought of

Bergson denounces and rejects the metamorphosis of time into space, Proust not only accommodates himself to it, but installs himself in it, carries it to extremes, and makes of it finally one of the principles of his art. This is what the following short essay intends to show. To the bad juxta-position, to the intellectual space condemned by Bergson, there is opposed a good juxtaposition, an aesthetic space, where, in ordering themselves, moments and places form the work of art, altogether memorable and admirable.

IN TERMS of the title it bears, one knows that the Proustian novel is very exactly a "search for lost time." A being sets out in quest of his past, makes every effort to rediscover his preceding existence. Thus one sees the hero awakening in the middle of the night and asking himself to what epoch of his life there is attached this moment in which he recovers consciousness. This is a moment totally deprived of any connection with the rest of duration, a moment suspended in itself, and profoundly anguished, because the one who lives it does not literally know *when* he lives. Lost in time, he is reduced to an entirely momentary life.

But the ignorance of this awakened sleeper is much graver than it seems. If he does not know *when* he lives, he no longer knows *where* he lives. His ignorance is no less important as to his position in space than as to his position in duration: "And when I awakened in the middle of the night, as I was *ignorant as to where I found myself,* I did not know in the first instant who I was."[1]

The first question that comes to the lips of the Proustian being is, then, no different from that posed at the end by so many of the characters of Marivaux, fallen, as they recognize it willingly, from the moon, and asking themselves in what place and in what moment they find themselves: "I am lost," they say; "my head spins; where am I?" These heedless and charming people do not know where they are; they are all astray, because, in their distraction or their passion, they have lost touch with the world that was theirs. Or, rather—we are on a tragic plane, and in a way of life that hardly resembles Marivaudian heedlessness— the ignorance of the Proustian person is more precisely comparable to the state of mind of that being which Pascal imagines transported, while sleeping, to a desert isle, and awaking there in the morning, in terror, "not knowing where he is, nor the means of getting out."

The being who awakes and who, upon awaking, recovers consciousness of his existence, recovers also consciousness of a span of life singularly and tragically shrunken. Who is he? He no longer knows, and he no longer knows because he has lost the means of relating the place and the moment in which he now lives to all the other places and moments of his former existence. His thought stumbles between times and between places. This moment in which he breathes, is it contiguous to a moment of his infancy, his adolescence, his adulthood? The place where he is, what is it? Is it his bedroom in Combray, or Paris, or one of those hotel rooms, grimmest of all, because, lacking all habitual sympathy with the being who occupies them, they are not real places, they hold nothing personal; they are, so to speak, anywhere in space? On the other hand, for him who awakes in the night, how can he be sure how the place disposes itself? "For an instant," writes Proust in the preface to *Contre Sainte-Beuve*, "I was like those sleepers who on awaking in the night do not know where they find themselves, do not know in what bed, in what house, in what place on earth, in what year of their life they find themselves."[2] Thus, groping, the mind seeks to situate itself. But it has "lost the plan of the place where it finds itself."[3] At random, in the dark, one places the window here, on the opposite side the door; up until the moment when there comes a ray of light, which, making the room clearer, constrains the window to leave its place and to be replaced by the door. So that as chance directs, the order of places rotates and realigns itself from bottom to top. Or as it happened in another episode, in the very same place where the wall of his room rose, the hero, still a child, sees another space appear, a moor on which a horseman rides. But the first space is not abolished; the body of the horseman coincides with the doorknob. Two spaces can then superimpose themselves, the one on the other, as if there were "a wavering and momentary stained window."[4] Now this vacillation, this vertigo, how many times has one not seen it affect the Proustian personage! It comes even when, being fully awake, he is disturbed by an unexpected event. For example, when at the end of an invitation Marcel reads the unhoped-for signature of Gilberte, he cannot believe his eyes; he does not know where he is: "With a vertiginous swiftness this improbable signature played at puss in the corner with my bed, with my chimney, with my wall. *I saw everything waver,* as does someone who falls from a horse."[5]

Wavering of the wall where the child sees Golo astride a horse; wavering of the room where the adolescent receives the first mark of interest from his loved one; wavering, finally, of the room in which the anguished adult awakens in the night. Here are three examples of a dizziness, both interior and exterior, psychical and spatial, which, in three distinct epochs of his existence, affects at one and the same time the mind of the hero and the very places where he finds himself in these three moments. But these moments of vertigo are not the only ones. One remembers the singular episode of the three trees on the way to Hudimesnil. Strange and familiar, never before seen, and yet similar to some image of the past the mind cannot identify again, the paramnesic phenomenon experienced by the mind forbids the thought "to recognize them in the place from which they seemed, so to speak, detached," as well, moreover, to situate them in some other place; so that, adds Proust, "my mind having stumbled between some far off year and the present moment, *the environs of Balbec were wavering.* . . ."[6]

What wavers here is not only time but place. It is space. A place tries to substitute itself for another place; to take its place. It is the same in an episode even more memorable. At the end of *Le temps retrouvé,* at the house of the Prince of Guermantes, the hero touches his lips with a strongly starched napkin. At once, he says, there surges the dining room at Balbec, "trying to shake the solidity of the House of Guermantes," and "making for an instant all the armchairs waver around me."[7] In a word, just as the bedroom at Combray and the landscape of Golo on horseback, Balbec and the Hotel de Guermantes are vacillating and substitutionable. As do the wall and the moor, they contend for the same place. They are one too many; one usurps the place of the other. The phenomenon of Proustian memory has then not only the effect of making the mind totter between two distinct epochs; it forces it to choose between two mutually incompatible places. The resurrection of the past, says Proust in substance, forces our mind to "oscillate" between years long past and the present time "in the dizziness of an uncertainty like that which one experiences sometimes before an ineffable vision at the moment of going to sleep."[8]

At the moment of going to sleep, at the inverse and corresponding moment of awaking, in the chiaroscuro wherein the consciousness is less prepared to withstand the phenomena that trouble it, the Proustian personage sometimes sees space split up, divided in two, losing its apparent simplicity and immobility. And it can be that this experience should have, for him who experiences it, a vertiginous happiness. But most of the time, the discovery of the unstable character of places inspires in him, completely on the contrary, a feeling of apprehension and even of horror: "Perhaps the immobility of things about us," writes Proust, "is imposed by our certainty that they are themselves and not others, by the immobility of our thought in face of them. The fact remains that each time I awoke thus, my mind agitating itself, in order to find out, without succeeding, where I was, everything was whirling about me, in the dark: things, countries, years."[9]

"Trying to know where I was. . . ." We see clearly then, from the first moment—one could almost say also: from the first *place*—in the account, the work of Proust asserts itself as a search not only for lost time, but also for lost space. The one is like the other, lost in the same manner, in the sense one says he has lost his way and looks for his road. But lost also in the sense one says he has lost his baggage, lost like the beads of a necklace that is broken. How to string together again the place where one is, the moment when one lives, to all the other moments and places that are scattered all along a vast expanse? One could say that space is a sort of undeterminable milieu where places wander in the same fashion that in cosmic space the planets wander. Yet the movement of the planets is calculable. But how does one calculate the movement of places that are wandering? Space does not frame them; it does not assign them one unchangeable position. As happens sometimes in the images of our thought, nothing contests the fact, says Proust, that a piece of landscape brought to the shore of today, "detaches itself so completely from everything, that it floats uncertain in my thought like a flowering Delos, without my being able to say from what country, from what time—perhaps, very simply, from what dream— it comes."[10]

Delight of seeing the image of a place of which we cannot determine the origin move in our mind, like a beautiful ship without a home port. But most often anguish, the anguish of seeing the mobility of places aggravate still more the mobility, already so frightening in itself, of our being. For how is one not to lose his faith in life, when he perceives that the only fixity he believed he found there—

a fixity of places, a fixity of objects that are situated there—
is illusory? The mobility of places takes away our last
shelter. It raises our anchor. To what are we able to cling,
if, like times and like beings, places are also swept on in
this course that can lead only to death?

Finally, the mobility of places has as a consequence the
respective isolation of these places, the ones in relation
to the others. If places move about, unless they do so at
the same speed and go in the same direction (but alas! we
know on the contrary that their courses are essentially
aberrant!) forcibly there must change also the apparently
constant relationships that linked them to other places
and that made of space a network of stable correspondences
and proportions. The distance from Paris to Balbec varies;
that from Balbec to Raspelière also. In brief, the absence
or the reinforcing of habits, the attention or the distraction,
the fear or the confidence, or, more simply, the substitu-
tion of one mode of locomotion for another, sometimes
lengthens and sometimes shortens the roads we travel.
But also, now and then, a more serious thing, there is no
longer any road; the place where one is leads to no other
places; it is like an island, isolated on all sides, incapable of
prolonging the network of its vanished communications.
A place broken off from the rest of the world, which subsists in itself and of itself, like a besieged citadel; a place
situated in absence, as a negation or a lack of access to
other places; a place that finally seems absolutely *lost* in
the solitude of space: "Having no more any universe, nor
any bedroom, nor body, except threatened by the enemies
which were surrounding me, except invaded to the bone by
fever, I was alone; I wanted to die."[11]

The being bereft of place is deprived of a universe, without a fireside, without fire and abode. He is, so to speak, nowhere; or rather, he is it matters not where; a sort of floating waif in the emptiness of hollow waves. But also, what joy, what relief for him, when all at once his vertigo ceases, the walls stop turning around and around, the floating images regain their habitual fixity! Twice, in Proust's novel, there occurs an episode in which the author has exactly transposed, in the realm of space, this victory over the destructive forces of time, which precisely in its essence constitutes the novel. There is first the account of a familiar walk at Combray, where everyone except the father has lost the sense of orientation, so that, like an awakened sleeper, nobody knows where he is. But then, just at the moment when anguish should begin, and the uneasy question of the stray one: Where am I? is ready to spring to his lips, the author, through the mediation of the father, consents this time to express a reassuring answer: "Suddenly my father stopped and asked my mother: 'Where are we?' Exhausted by the walk, but proud of him, she confessed to him tenderly that she had no idea at all. He would shrug his shoulders and laugh. Then, as if he had brought it from his vest pocket with his key, he would point right in front of us to the little gate of our back garden, which had come with the corner of the Street of the Holy Spirit, to wait for us at the end of those unknown paths."[12]

If familiar places can then sometimes give us up, they can also come back to us, and, to our great relief, can reoccupy their earlier site. As can be seen, these places behave exactly as the moments of the past, as memories.

They leave; they return. And in the same way as in certain epochs of our existence, suddenly, without cause, without voluntary effort on our part, we regain lost time; just so, in the same apparently fortuitous fashion, thanks to the intervention of some providence or other, the person, wandering as he was in space, finds himself at home, and regains, at the same time, his lost place.

Thus we must pay particular attention to a second episode of the same kind, which, according to his method, Proust has placed further on in his book, in order to recall and deepen what has already been cited.

In the course of a musical evening at Madame Verdurin's, the young hero finds himself astray amidst a music entirely new to him in the heart of a country whose paths he does not know: "The concert began. I did not know what they were playing; I found myself in an unknown country. Where could I situate it? In the work of what composer did I find myself?"

Then, like a genie or a fairy from the *Thousand and One Nights,* whose benevolent intervention would dissipate the uncertainties of the listener, or like the father, who, during the walk in Combray, would reassure and inform his lost family, a magic apparition, says Proust, comes to assist the hero and to answer the implicit question he had asked. Now let us listen carefully to the terms in which the author retraces for us this conjuncture: "As when, in a country one does not claim to know, and where in fact one has arrived from a new direction, after having turned up a new road, one finds oneself all at once emerging onto another whose even the lesser nooks are familiar, but only one hasn't the habit of traveling there, one suddenly says to oneself: 'But it is the little path that leads to the little gate of the garden of my friends. I am two minutes from their place'; Thus, suddenly, I recognized myself in the midst of this music that was new to me. I was in the middle of Vinteuil's Sonata."[13]

Is there any need to hold that the similitude between those two passages can only be intended by the author? Too many details are alike, up to the little gate that opens into the garden of Aunt Léonie, and that of certain friends. No doubt, in the first of these two passages, it is a question of persons lost in exterior space; in the other, it is a question of a being lost in the midst of an interior space. But in the one case, just as in the other, the essential issue is the discovery of place. To discover the little gate at the end of the garden is to discover a place that is no longer drifting in space, but that has its place in our memories, and that bears a name. The person who was lost somewhere in the universe discovers himself abruptly in a familiar territory where nothing has changed. To find again the lost place is then, if not the same thing, at least something very similar to recovering lost time. When in the depth of memory, some image of the past offers itself confusedly to the consciousness, there still remains a task to be accomplished: which consists, says Proust, "in learning what particular circumstance, what epoch of the past is in question."[14] This task bears a name. It is called *localization.*[15] Now, in the same way that the mind localizes a remembered image in duration, it localizes it in space. It is not only a certain period of its childhood that the Proustian being sees rise up from his cup of tea; it is also a room, a church, a town, a solid topographical whole, which no longer wanders, which no longer wavers.

WHETHER IT BE by grace of memory, by an act of the imagination, or simply by reason of the faith by which we attach ourselves to certain sites, the latter are set to differ from all the others; they stand apart in the spaces of our mind. Places found again in the depth of our memory; places created in us by our dreams, or by participation in the dreamings of others, which is one of the effects of art; or yet, but more rarely, places directly perceived by us in their particular beauty and enriched by the presence of a being who confers upon them something of his own individuality—with Proust, there is a diversity of places, unmingled with others, which seem to live within their frontiers an absolutely independent life. Such is their essential characteristic. From the external world to themselves, there is not this natural topographical continuity that is found everywhere between one place and other places. From the moment one perceives them, on the contrary, one gets the clear idea that they do not extend into the surrounding universe, that they are separate from it. There is, for example, not far from Raspelière a certain landscape of forest and shingles: "One instant, the denuded rocks by which I was surrounded, the sea, which one perceived through their clefts, *floated before my eyes like the fragments of another universe.*"[16]

Another universe, into whose enclosed space one penetrates, not only as one would pass from this to that point of ordinary space, but from a local manner of existing to a manner fundamentally different, or as, in withdrawing into oneself, one is transported from places forming part of the exterior world to those purely ideal places which have their reality only within our mind. And, indeed, in the case cited, that is precisely so, and in two distinct fashions, since it appears in the story that the place in question is nothing but a landscape, by means of which the painter Elstir was inspired of old to depict scenes of fabulous subjects that had strongly struck the imagination of our hero when he had seen them: "Their recollection brought the places where I found myself so far *from the real world,* that I would not have been surprised . . . if I had in the course of my walk come across a mythological personage."[17]

Here then the placing apart of a fragment of space, its isolation in regard to the real world, is the result of art, but of an art seen again across memory. Poets and artists have the power of giving us access to "some marvelous sites, different from the rest of the world."[18] And that not only in the general characteristics which these places present, but even in certain concrete details that make such a route, such a nook of a garden, such a bend of river "appear to us other and more beautiful than the rest of the world."[19]

A miracle that music also produces, and that is effected by the little phrase of Vinteuil, when, by a play of perspectives, it allows itself to be glimpsed, unexpected and delightful, at the end of a whole sonorous development: "And as in those pictures of Pieter de Hooch, deepened by the narrow frame of a door half-opened, far away, of a different color, in the velvet softness of interposed light, the little phrase appeared dancing, pastoral, inserted, episodic, belonging to another world."[20]

It sometimes happens that the place that sets itself in contrast to all others appears *beyond* the others, not, indeed, to continue them, but, on the contrary, to mark the quality that makes them belong to another world. But it is also possible that the privileged place, far from standing out against that which surrounds it, differs from it only by certain nuances, it is true, essential, informing us by this mingling of familiar and unhabitual traits, that it is used as intermediary between the world as we know it, and another world that is quite strange and far-off. It is as if then the landscape—shall we say perceived or dreamed of?—went to make up a sort of avenue, which it sufficed simply to follow, in order to pass from one universe to the other, whether one passes from external perception to reminiscence, from tangible reality to imaginary space, or from objective verity to that of art.

There is an admirable example of this in a "landscape" in *Jean Santeuil*, where, in a movement very rare for him, the novelist addresses the reader:

> And you too, older than Jean, reader, of the enclosure of

a garden situated on a height, have you not had sometimes the feeling that it was not only other fields, other trees that extended before you, but a certain country under its special sky? These few trees that came up to the enclosure you had been leaning on were like the real trees of the first plan of a panorama; they served as a *transition* between what you knew, the garden where you had come to visit, and that unreal, mysterious thing, a land that lay before you under the appearances of plains, developing richly in valleys, letting the light play upon itself. Here are still real things . . . but farther away there is something else. . . .[21]

Sometimes, then, there is opened before us a road that leaves our habitual places, but that, insidiously, without our being able to render a clear account of the place where it passes an invisible frontier, leads us toward other places situated outside of our universe. It is thus that the walk of the Guermantes Way begins normally enough along the course of the Vivonne, but, for him who would pursue it up to the sources of this river, ends in a place no less abstract and ideal than the Gates of Hades.[22] And thus it is again that the corridor in which the Prince of Saxe is engaged in order to join in her theater box his cousin Guermantes, seems to branch off from the banal place occupied by the hero, a witness to this conjuncture, on "an eventual passage toward a new world," and "to lead the way to marine grottoes, and to the mythological kingdom of the nymphs of waters."[23]

A long time before Alain-Fournier, Proust had thus conceived the idea of an intermediary center connecting universes of different species. But different from Fournier, the intermediary center does not present itself in Proust in the form of a "real" road, uniting two determined points

on the map. Let us rather say that with Proust this center
or road is the topological representation of the very act by
which the mind transports what it sees, and makes the
objects of the real pass into the imaginary: "Elstir could
look at a flower," writes Proust, "only if he transplanted it
first into the interior garden where we are forced to live
always."[24] —Interior gardens where we transplant not only
flowers, but also landscapes, the shape of human beings,
and the very names they carry. Interior places, which are
truly different from all others, because, like the church of
Combray, they possess another dimension and because we
can only represent them to ourselves across a certain
depth of duration.

There is nothing less objective, then, than genuine
Proustian places; genuine places, those which are invariably
connected with certain human presences. There is never,
in fact, with Proust, a place described without in the foreground, the profile of such or such a figure; in the same
way that there never appears in Proust a figure without the
presence of a framework ready to insert and support it.
Invariably it is in a landscape minutely circumscribed that
the Proustian personage shows itself for the first time.

From the moment it appears, this place, associating
itself with him, gives him a note as distinct and recognizable
as a Wagnerian *leitmotiv*. Yes, no doubt, in what follows
the personage will reappear elsewhere. But he will not cease
to be bound to the primitive site in our memory. It is of
this that we are reminded from the very first moment; it is
this that we see unfold, unfold promptly, in whatever
spot the personage finds himself; as if he had been fixed in
a painting more revealing than anything else, where he will

always be showing up against the same background.

It is thus with all Proustian personages. How to recall, for example, Gilberte, or rather the image the hero has formed of her, if not under the aspect of a little girl, accompanied by an old gentleman, and silhouetting herself with him against the background of the cathedrals they visit by turn. "Most often now when I thought of her, *I saw her before the porch of a cathedral,* explaining to me the significance of the statues, and with a smile that spoke kindly of me, introducing me as her friend to Bergotte."[25] How on the other hand, to imagine Saint-Loup or Albertine otherwise than against the marine landscape of Balbec. "He came from the beach, and the sea, which filled up to mid-height the stained glass of the hall, *gave him a background against which he could detach himself full length.*"[26] Thus there is fixed before our eyes, inserted in his context, the image of the future friend of Marcel. Now it is the same for the "young girls in flower," and for the principal one of these: Albertine. "It was to them that my thought was pleasantly suspended when I fancied I was thinking of some other thing, or of nothing. But when, not thinking at all, I thought of them, more unconsciously still, they formed for me the hilly and blue waves of the sea, the profile of a procession before the sea."[27]

Profile of a group, profile of a single face: "Was she not in fact the young girl I had seen for the first time at Balbec under her flat beret with her eyes intent and laughing, mysterious still, *slim like a silhouette profiled upon the wave?*"[28]

Whatever the images may be, ceaselessly denied and substituting themselves for each other, that she will present in succession, Albertine will not be able to obliterate this first image, fantastically cast off by her lover on a seascape of clouds and waves. First image; last image, or almost so. For not much time before vanishing, saying goodbye to him one evening, Albertine, he says, held out her hand to him with the abrupt motion she had used in those first times on the beach at Balbec: "This forgotten movement restored to the body to which it gave life the form of Albertine, which hardly knew me at all. It gave back to Albertine, ceremoniously under an air of abruptness, her first newness, her unknownness, and *even her true frame. I saw the sea behind that young girl.*"[29]

Thus, for Proust, human beings appear located in certain places that give them support and outline, and that determine the perspective according to which one is allowed to see them. A singular thing, this novelist of interiority invariably obliges himself to present his personages (except for one central consciousness) under the aspect of exteriority. Human beings are silhouettes that are outlined, shapes that fall under one's gaze. But still that is not enough to say. Not only are the personages bound to their appearances; it is necessary that their appearances be tied to a local environment that frames them and serves them, so to speak, like a jewel box. To this first framework others will come to add themselves, or to substitute themselves, as time goes on. Thus the Proustian being will appear, by turn, in a series of sites; just like persons who make themselves into a series of portraits, where one sees them, with a background that is always different: for example, a garden in the country, a wall covered with bills, a drawing room, a station platform, etc. But if, with Proust, a person is always put in a place, he is never, or very rarely described *between* places. It is as if it depended upon a witnessing look, which watched him more often than not installed in one of the diverse spots, from the one to the other of which it is necessary to suppose that he is transported; without, for all that, the eye of the author being capable or desirous of following the movement by which he goes from the one to the other. So that what here is found only rarely revealed is the continuous progression of beings in their physical as in their moral life, the motives that impel them to abandon their old frameworks in order to give themselves new ones. In brief, the only images of themselves Proustian personages are permitted to offer us are similar to those photographs of the same person, of which our albums are full. Such a person in such an epoch of his life, and then in such another; such a person in the country, in the city, in evening dress, in lounging clothes. Each of these "photos" is rigorously determined by its framework; the whole is discontinuous. Nevertheless, the association of each person to a certain place on which he is profiled has for effect the conferring upon it, if not the continuity that it lacks, at least one aspect that is eminently concrete. Beings surround themselves with the places where they find themselves, the way one wraps oneself up in a garment that is at one and the same time a disguise and a characterization. Without places, beings would be only abstractions. It is places that make their image precise and that give them the necessary support, thanks to which we can assign them a place in our mental space, dream of them, and remember them.

Proustian persons never let themselves be evoked without their being accompanied by the image of sites that they have successively occupied. Sites, moreover, that are not necessarily only those where they have really appeared. For to the series of real places where the hero remembers to have seen them there is added the image of the places where—even before they were encountered in flesh and bone—the hero dreamed of seeing them.

Each being is thus placed by us, not only in one place, but in a system of places, of which certain ones are real, and others imaginary. This is true for Gilberte, for Albertine, for the Duchess of Guermantes:

> Each of the women I have known did rise at a different point of my life, set up as a divinity, as a local protectress, first in the midst of a landscape that was dreamed, whose juxtaposition checkered my life and where I was pledged to imagine it; and afterwards seen from the side of memory, surrounded by sites where I had known her, of which she reminded me by staying attached to them. For if our life is vagabond, our memory is sedentary, and it is in vain that we dash forward; our memories, shored to places from which we detach ourselves, continue to pursue there their domestic life. . . .[30]

Infallibly, then, with Proust, in reality as in dream, persons and places are united. The Proustian imagination would not know how to conceive beings otherwise than in placing them against a local background that plays for them the part of foil and mirror. To evoke a human being, this act so simple, which is the first act of the novelist composing his work, is tantamount with Proust to rendering a form visible and putting it in a framework. It is a trick of mind veritably essential, and which, with Proust, can be noticed not only in his novels, but in his critical writings and ideological essays, and even in his correspondence.

It is thus that writing to the pretty actress Louisa de Mornand, then absent from Paris, Proust gives himself up to the pleasure of imagining her in the place where she spends her vacation: "How much I would love to walk with you in these streets of Blois, which must be for your beauty a charming framework. It is an old framework, a Renaissance framework. But it is also a new framework, since I have never seen you in it. And in new places, people we love seem to have some sort of renewal. To see your beautiful eyes reflect the light sky of Touraine, your exquisite shape stand out against the background of the old castle, would be more moving for me than to see you in another dress. This would be to see you in new attire."[31]

So that, by the grace of a momentary association, the beautiful eyes, the exquisite shape of the actress receive from the surrounding landscape a supplementary charm. But the inverse is equally true. If the place enriches the being who is found there, the being confers on the place where it is found something of its own individuality. "Thus in the depths of a landscape palpitated the charm of a being. So, in a being, all of a landscape invested its poetry."[32] This phrase from *Contre Sainte-Beuve* already defines and prefigures the reciprocity of exchanges, which, in *A la recherche du temps perdu,* occurs between persons and places. Sometimes it seems that the place has so much need of a being that it is ready to engender it, to draw it out of its own substance, by a creative act identical to the one by which emanate from it flowers, trees, stones, houses, all the objects that constitute or furnish it: "The passer-by who aroused my desire seemed to be no model whatsoever of this general type: woman, *but a natural and necessary product of this soil.*"[33] Sometimes, on the contrary, it is the human object that seems to need to complete or enlarge itself by becoming the central point of a geographic reality: "I always imagined, situated about the woman I loved the places I then desired the most . . . I would have wished that this would be she who made me visit them, who opened for me the access to an unknown world."[34]

Place, then, opens out to receive woman; but the image of woman opens out also to receive place. Of this curious interdependence, at once topological and anthropological, the best example is certainly that of *names.* Family names, country names, one knows the immense role they play in the Proustian work, a role so great that entire parts of it receive their title from them, and in a sense, it would not be an exaggeration to consider the whole novel itself as one vast amplification on the influence exercised by names on the mind. But family names and especially noble family names have this particularity, of being at one and the same time the name of a place and the name of a person, and of amalgamating thus into one unique identity the two ingredients of which the Proustian imagination has need. Of this mental alchemy realized by the name there are in Proust numerous examples.

That of the Duchess of Guermantes: "The Duchess of Guermantes had seated herself. Her name, as it was accompanied by her title, added to her physical person her duchy, which projected itself around her, and made prevail the shady gold coolness of the Woods of Guermantes right in the middle of the drawing room, around the ottoman where she sat."[35]

Besides the name of the Duchess, there is another name, less known in the novel, but hardly less evocative:

> The name of the Prince of Faffenheim-Munsterburg-Weiningen kept in the freedom with which its first syllables were—as one says in music—attacked, and in the stammering repetition that scanned them, the dash, the affected artlessness, the ungainly German "daintinesses" projected, like greenish branches, on the "Heim" of dark blue enamel, which displayed the mysteriousness of a Rhenish stained glass window behind the pale and delicately chiseled gildings of the German eighteenth century. This name contained among the various names from which it had been formed, that of a little German watering-place where as a child I had been with my grandmother. . . . Thus, under the visor of the Prince of the Holy Empire, and of the equerry of Franconia, it was the face of a beloved land where often there froze for me the rays of the six o'clock sun that I saw. . . .[36]

The name is thus simultaneously individual and local. It is the name of country on the same grounds that it is the name of person and the name of family. But it is even more. Under the form of one of those phenomena which one uses to transport objective realities into the mental world, it is this original topological entity (issued from the fusion of a real site with the image of a person or of the history of a family) that is an unreal place, since it has no place in the external space; but subjectively real, since it is situated in the spaces of the mind: "It is still today one of great charms of titled families that they seem situated in a particular *corner* of earth, that their *name* is always a *name* of place, or that the name of their country seat (and it is again often the same) gives automatically to the imagination the impression of settled residence and at the same time the desire of travel. Each titled name contains in the colored space of its syllables a country house where, after a difficult road, arrival is sweet on a gay winter's evening."[37]

What is most often the Proustian snobbery? A revery on place names and noble families. Thanks to the colors whose names enrich them, to the thousand nuances of concrete humanity, which, by the agency of names, come to give them a particular countenance; places are set to play in the imagination of men a role no different from precisely that played by human people. Their marvels and mysteries become personal marvels and mysteries. Bearers of a name that humanizes and individualizes them, they show themselves and disappear, hide certain secrets, inspire certain desires, unveil certain beauties. Thus places merit being the object of our admiring curiosity and even of our love: "Places are persons," Proust writes somewhere.[38] And elsewhere he insists: "Names present persons—and towns, which we get used to believing individual, unique as persons, a confusing image that draws from their dazzling sonority or their shadow the color by which they are uniformly painted. . . ."[39] One is reminded of the grand movement of desire and dream unlatched in the mind of the young hero of *A la recherche du temps perdu* by the perspective of a journey to Italy. An infinite power of suggestion is revealed in the names of Florence and Venice, endowing these still unknown cities with a crowd of particularities intensely individual, though quite imaginary. It is that the hero, as Proust says, is still at an

age when "we believe with a profound faith in the originality and in the individual life of the place where we find
ourselves."[40]

Of the place where we find ourselves; of the place, so
much more, of which we dream. If there is, in fact, something significant in the Proustian topology, it is indeed the
insistence with which the novelist returns to the originality
and individuality of the character that places present—as
well indeed the places conceived by interpretative thought,
as those perceived in sensible experience and reviewed
later in the memory. "There is something individual in
places,"[41] recognized Proust. And some lines later, he speaks
of "landscapes with which sometimes the night, in its
dreams, embrace him with an almost fantastic power."[42]

"This *unique* thing that a place is. . . ."[43] The charm of
a place, then, in the last analysis, is the fact that it is
itself and not another; that it possesses, as much as human
beings do, this essential characteristic that is called
uniqueness. Just as Swann is Swann, and Albertine,
Albertine (in such a way that it would be the gravest
error for him who would like to understand these persons
to search out in them only the most general traits that
they share with all other representatives of the human
species) just as much so, Venice is Venice, and Florence,
Florence; and if it is undeniable that these places are
bound to other places, to Italy, to Europe, to space, this
abstract liaison that exists between all the points of
extension would not help us to penetrate what is exclusively Florentine in Florence, and what is exclusively
Venetian in Venice. Each place reveals itself as the seat
of an absolutely original reality. Each place has, so to

speak, nothing in common with other places, even with those that adjoin it. In brief, the Proustian conception of the radical originality of places neglects precisely the only characteristic that would permit *knowing them together:* the fact that places participate in the same space, and are placed at a greater or lesser distance, the ones from the others, but always measureable, on the same map.

Places are not able to be reduced to pure localization in space, no more than Charlus and Norpois, Françoise and M. de Bréauté, the Duke of Guermantes and the Grandmother of Marcel are able to be regarded simply as interchangeable specimens of the human race. For beings are persons, and persons can be understood only through their own originality. Now one sees that it is the same with places. Places are islands in space, monads, in "minute universes set apart."[44] And the sole generality that matters in them is not at all the anonymous generality that is found in all the points of extent, but the identity that is noticed between similar types of landscapes whose resemblance strikes us despite the distance, and offers us "the consistency of a particular type of pleasure and of almost a framework of existence."[45]

LIKE WORKS by the same painter on display at different museums of Europe, a whole series of Proustian sites seem thus to proclaim their belonging to a single universe. But these sites or pictures have been separated, the ones from the others, by great neutral distances, in such a way that the first aspect suggested by the work of Proust is that of a very incomplete ensemble, where the number of subsisting traces is largely surpassed by the number of gaps. Rarely does the representation of things there appear total or panoramic. It is nearly always fragmentary, now larger, now narrower, but most often reduced, whether it be by some obstruction, or more often, by some "fracture" in the field of vision—to a section of the real, strictly limited, beyond which it is hopeless to try to see anything. In brief, the most exact image of the Proustian universe is no different from that image of Combray which appears at the beginning of Proust's tale: *"a sort of luminous wall looming up on the midst of indistinct shadows* like those that the flaming up of a Bengal light or some electrical projection brightens up and *divides into sections* in an edifice of which all other parts remain immersed in night."[46]

True, the brief miracle of the affective memory will be able to have as a consequence the completing of certain parts of the picture. But this miracle is itself intermittent. Its efficacy is of worth for only the very moment when it operates; what it restores is restituted only in a provisory fashion, so that the partial restoration realized by the memory has for effect only the substituting for the spatial discontinuity, a discontinuity this time temporal. Thus one can say of the entire work of Proust what in the *Plaisirs et les jours* he himself said of a certain epoch of his life, that it was *"a progress interrupted by gaps."*[47] Gaps which prevent the pieces from joining, from forming a succession. That is more particularly true of the personages in the Proustian novel, that one never perceives them except from such and such an angle, replaced just as fast by another. Albertine is the best example of this, Albertine infinitely divided into multiple aspects of herself, so that she presents "a splitting up into numerous parts, numerous Albertines. . . ."[48]

To the dividing of beings into fractions there is added the parceling out of things, of works, and even of thoughts. One knows that the Proustian macrocosm holds up a small number of microcosms that are the mental universes of certain artists, but of these interior universes one again sees no more than the fragments. The Proustian universe is a universe in pieces, of which the pieces contain other pieces, those, also, in their turn, other pieces. Thus the world of Elstir, appearing at intervals in the novel, but never in a continuous fashion, exists only there under the form of a series of works—scattered over a studio, in galleries, in particular collections, as well as, moreover, in some rare landscapes, disseminated here and there, in the external reality—that are Elstir's in the sense that they have served him as models. In the same way, for Proust, the pictures of Vermeer are "the fragments of a selfsame world,"[49] just as the universe of Vinteuil subsists only in *"disjointed fragments, bursts of the scarlet fractures* of an unknown festival of color."[50]

There are many causes of this fragmentation of the Proustian universe. Certainly one among them, and not the least, is the intermittent character of memory, and, in a general fashion, of all the feelings. This is not the only cause, nor perhaps the most important one. The temporal discontinuity is itself preceded, indeed even commanded, by a discontinuity still more radical, that of space. Both are mutually intermingled and augmented in so inextricable a fashion that perhaps it would be useful here to make some reflections on what is found implicated in Proust, by that which cannot be called otherwise than a general principle of discontinuity.

One would have to say that inevitably there is discontinuity where there is heterogeneity, or, what amounts to the same thing, that the first discontinuity, the source of all the others, is the discontinuity of essences. In a world like that of pantheism (Bruno, Spinoza) where everything, in the final count, is authenticated as participant in the most complete unity of substance, there is no discontinuity; there is only the appearance of it. In a world like that of science, there is no more any discontinuity, but for the opposite reason, because there is no essence. Everything is reduced to a quantitative enumeration that supposes the presence of the homogeneous on all sides. On this point, Bergson has made all the necessary distinctions.

But the world of Proust is the contrary of the world of scientists and differs no less from a world in which the unity of substance would reign. It is a world that affirms the qualitative and the heterogeneous. As soon as a thing manifests itself in its own quality, in its "essence," it reveals itself as different from all other things (and their essences). From it to the others there is no passage. Qualitative realities for Proust seem condemned then to an isolated, insular existence, separated by insurmountable distances.

So, if the Proustian world greatly differs from the Bergsonian one, it resembles, on the contrary, some others where quality also predominates; for instance, the world of Leibnitz. But what is exceptional and perhaps even veritably unique in Proust is the fact that this qualitativity is not at all confined in him to the world of objects and living things, but that it affects also, as we have seen, the world of space.

For most philosophers, space, still more than time, is the world of homogeneity. "L'espace à soi pareil," as Mallarmé said, space always identical to itself, This is so because, ordinarily, for the philosopher, space is what is prior to places, what *a priori* is already there to contain or hold them. Whatever places are, in whatever concrete way they show themselves, mind conceives, behind them, below them, all around them, a bare anonymous reality, abstract, totally devoid of characteristics, which presents itself as the impersonal ground where places stand out and distribute themselves. Thus the concrete world would take its place in the abstract, the personal in the impersonal, and the heterogeneous in the homogeneous. First of all there would be space, and then the places that would take their position in space.

Perhaps it would not be unhelpful to remark here that such a conception of space has for a consequence to establish the *a posteriori* nature, and therefore also the contingent and secondary characters of all discontinuity. Since there would be primarily continuity—which is space—discontinuity could not be understood except as the subsequent event that, accidentally and probably temporarily, came to disturb an order undeniably initial and promising to be eternal. Of all necessity, the principle of spatial continuity has as a corollary a corresponding principle, which is the principle of the continuity of time.

Such is the habitual optic of all philosophy of space. It can emerge only as an affirmation of the continuous, which is space.

But one cannot imagine anything that would be farther from Proustian thought. Not that the latter develops at any point, in theoretical or critical fashion, its point of view. Assuredly Proust had never dreamed of opposing his reflections on space to those of current philosophy, and it is entirely likely to suppose that he had no consciousness of his disagreement with it. It is rather that we are here not on the level of speculative thought, but on that of an experience that is drawn from itself, without raising itself,

save rarely, to the metaphysical generalization of its dis-
coveries. But on this plane, which is the one where
Proust naturally set himself up, there is never a question
of space; there is only the question of places, and the
distance that exists between places.

It is true that the word distance can be taken as a
synonym of space. Nevertheless, with Proust, distance is
never a space that lengthens, that lets in, that links, that
fills up a void. It is this void, only this void. Distance is
space, but space stripped of all positivity, space without
force, without efficacy, without power of fullness of
coordination and unification. Instead, a sort of general
simultaneity that would be developed from all sides to
support, contain, and connect beings together; space is
very simply here an incapacity that is manifested everywhere, in all the objects of the world, to form together
an order. Things are, but they are *at a distance.* A distance
which it is impossible for them to suppress or reduce.
In the Proustian universe, at this stage, it is never allowed
to draw near, to touch, to establish ones with others, in
the intimacy of neighborhood. All that is living in it is
living in solitude. And the feeling of distance, which, under
one form or another, never ceases to manifest itself, con-
founds itself with the anguished feeling of existence. At
the bottom of all desires there is an impotency, inherent
in the very nature of beings, that forbids their attaining
the object of their desires. To desire is to render apparent
a distance apart. To love is to see escape in the distance
the being one loves. It is to perceive, as Proust says, "those
frightful interior distances at the end of which a woman
we love appears to us to be so far away."[51] Distance for

Proust, then, can only be tragic. It is like the visible demonstration inscribed on infinite vastness, of the great principle of separation that affects and afflicts men. One is here. The loved one is there. Between these two points there is no bridge, no communication, nothing except a kind of tacit denial, universal and anonymous, opposed by space to that condition in people who draw near and join each other.

From the very first, in the work of Proust, the theme of distance, or negative space, attains the maximum of sorrowful intensity. It appears under the form of a goodnight kiss, desired by the child and refused by the mother, of a union between her and the child, which would abolish all distance. And the kiss refused is the absence substituting for the presence. Absence, source of anguish. What the nature of the latter is we know; it is, says Proust, the anguish there is in "feeling the one we love to be in a *place* of pleasure, where *we ourselves are not*."[52] Essentially, then, anguish holds to this nonidentity of the places respectively occupied by the being desired and the being who desires, to the distance abruptly perceived between the spot where one discovered oneself to be alone, and the place where he assumes that the other is and enjoys himself. Between the one and the other of these places, an abyss is revealed. Suddenly one understands that space is not a communicating milieu, a ground of union, a privileged zone where beings find themselves together. Suddenly one knows that space is exactly the contrary. Space is what sees to it that beings are obliged to live far away from each other. The one for whom the maternal kiss had been a gauge of a happy reunion, of a presence that Proust compares to the "divine presence,"[53] must resign himself to the inverse and terribly real evidence of absence.

Evidence which, the whole length of the Proust novel, is reiterated, and comes to making this an interminable demonstration of the impossibility for human beings to arrive at being present, the ones with the others. How many episodes have for their object the showing of distances, the rendering of absences visible. One sees it more particularly in two similar incidents where the main character is telephoning, the first time to his grandmother, the second to Albertine. In hearing in the depths of the receiver the voice of the loved person, he imagines for a moment absence conquered, distance suppressed. But immediately the illusion is dispelled:

> The voice of the dear person addresses itself to us. It is she, it is her voice that talks to us. She is there. But how far away she is! How many times had I not been able to listen without anguish. As if in front of this impossibility of seeing, before long hours of travel, her whose voice was so close to my ear, I felt better what was deceptive in the appearance of a most sweet nearness, and at what a distance we can be from persons *loved* at the moment when it seems that we shall have *only to extend a hand to hold them.* Real presence with this voice so near—in actual separation! but in anticipation also of an eternal separation.[54]

> But already, at the last words heard on the telephone, I began to understand that the life of Albertine was situated (though not materially) at such a distance from me that it would always be necessary for me to make fatiguing explorations to place my hands on hers, but even more, organized like field fortifications . . . existences disposed on five or six lines of folds, in such a way that, when one wished to see this woman, or to know her, one had come to strike too much to the right, too much to the left, too much ahead, or too much behind, and that one can, during months, years, never know anything.[55]

But the most admirable passage devoted by Proust to telephonic communication and its analogies is found in *Jean Santeuil*. It concerns the grandfather of Jean, M. Sandré, losing himself in his reveries, to his memories, and listening to the voice of his own past, which, in order to reach him, traverses "the long course of half a century":

> But at the moment when this beloved voice addresses itself to us in the telephone receiver, it seems to us to *feel*, as it were, a remoteness that leaps over us without having had the time to be felt. Thus when we rouse ourselves after several hours of drowsiness on the railroad, in the presence before us of new places that surround us, we feel, if not the fatigue, at least something like the vertigo of distances that the steam engine has traversed for us. . . . So the eyes of M. Sandré looked instantaneously at distant things, but the feeling of this atmosphere so long drawn out of days instantaneously traversed was nevertheless between those things and him.[56]

What then makes the illusory miracle of telephonic communication (and of its exact analogue, memory) is a presence at once regained and lost. Regained, because, despite the distance, and the forgetfulness, the presence returns to us; it makes itself be recognized by us; and nevertheless lost, because, in spite of the movement that brings it to our discovery, it remains nailed down to the place from whence it came, not budging an inch, in the depths of time, in the depths of space. And the instantaneous movement by which, on the telephone, from a place far away from us, a voice that is dear to us leaps over an immense interval only betrays the distance in which the person remains confined "at the end of the line," given that it is her voice alone that we are allowed to catch, while her being remains out of reach, on the other side of the abyss. Now it is the same for our memories. For if the sensory image they bring back to us seems to be transferred instantaneously to us, in devouring, as one says, distance, it is a past irremediably finished that they relate, a past that never ceases to be separated from us by the very distance, so that the latter, far from being suppressed, is on the contrary rendered more cruelly distinct by the movement of mnemonic thought, which, in traveling all the way, has more clearly revealed the length of time.

This length of time has the same extent as existence. The being who recollects an image of himself visible through all the depths of the past remembers also, in a sense, the interval that separates him from it. Thus already in a tale from the *Plaisirs et les jours,* the hero, recalling a certain epoch of his life, *calculates,* at one stroke, the interval; as if the memory were a reference mark, thanks to which the length of time of existence became not only visible but calculable: ". . . And he pitied himself as, so often, during *the whole length of his entire life,* he had perceived with compassion all his childhood."[57]

No doubt here, as in the episode cited from *Jean Santeuil,* as, still later, in so many other passages in *A la recherche du temps perdu,* the personage benefiting from the magical advantages of the affective memory suddenly finds himself in this exceptional situation in which the mind perceives what Baudelaire called the profundity of existence, and is then susceptible, in a sense, to "measuring" it. But, other the other hand, in interpreting these passages, we need to guard outselves from falling into a

double error. The first would consist in taking this profundity that reveals itself for a veritably positive existential
dimension; that is, for a continuity of memories overlapping
the ones upon the others, from the initial memory up to
the present moment, in such a way that they form an uninterrupted chain. There is nothing less positive, on the
contrary, than the temporal extent that reveals itself here.
It is not the entire life; it is only the "distance" perceived
when looking at this entire life. It is not a fullness but an
emptiness. The being who discovers here the profundity of
existence, discovers it in the emptiness of all existence. In
place of life remains the hollow left by life in withdrawing
itself.

On the other hand, there is nothing more ambiguous
than the word *calculation* applied to distance. It is not
inexact, in fact, as we shall see later, to conceive distance in
the Proustian sense of this term as a dimension analogous
to those of external space or of scientific time; provided
that, nevertheless, we did not consider it in fact as a mathe-
matical longness of life, measurable and convertible, for
example, in a determined number of stretches of space and
of years. The distance of which it is a question here has
nothing to do with quantity. If the contemplated or remembered object appears at a point from which the eye finds
itself separated by some neutral extent, no means can be
proposed to *compare* this particular distance to another
kind of distance, and thus to calculate the difference it
marks between subject and object. On the contrary, each
time that, with Proust, an image from the past or from the
outside rises from the depths of the mind, it is invariably
to give the impression of a reality perceived at the same

boundary point in a distance that could not diminish or increase. In other terms, distance here is *absolute*. Like a sculpture by Giacometti, which, in whatever spot where one goes to see it, presents the same slender silhouette, thus the object embraced by the Proustian regard seems unable to grow or to vanish; it can only offer itself there, where it is, vainly, out of reach: always afar, always outside, like an eternal stranger in an eternal absence.

iv

"THE MOST simple act or gesture remains locked in, as if in a thousand closed vases. . . ."[58]

"I open my eyes to the closed-in night, and I often ask myself if the hermetically sealed place where I am, lighted by electricity, is situated at Versailles rather than elsewhere, where I have not seen a single dead leaf whirl above any of its sheets of water."[59]

In brief, in Proust, with Proust, everything that lives, lives closed up in itself, and at the same time excluded from everything that is not itself. And this rigorous inclusion-exclusion, which splits existence in two, like a wall of which it is impossible to perceive at one and the same time the internal face and the external face, has for a result that on the one hand each being is exterior to all others, and nevertheless is enclosed within itself, without the possibility of communicating with the outside. Now this that is true of beings is equally true of moments and places. One knows with what persistence Proust returns to the Cartesian notion of a duration composed of independent moments, which, "the ones far from the others, unknowable one to another, remain in *closed vases* without communication between them on different afternoons."[60] But what is true of time is equally true of extensiveness. There are not only moments of time that are like closed vases; there are places in space. The famous distinction between the Guermantes Way and the Méséglise Way has no other object than to give of this parcelization an example as simple as possible and that nevertheless could be universally applied. Yes, it is true that there exist at Combray, like everywhere else, two "Ways" so different that it is impossible to go from the one to the other on the same day. But this impossibility that "encloses into the cell of distinct days" every afternoon, where necessarily one had to engage oneself only in one of two alternative directions, has for its immediate corollary the corresponding impossibility of being simultaneously engaged in the one *and* the other of two opposite directions. An impossibility that, this time, is properly spatial though it is bound to a temporal impossibility. I can find myself in such and such places only at different times, just as I can be in one same time only absent from the one or the other of those places. So that the unity of time implies the plurality of space, just as the unity of space implies the plurality of time. Any way that I turn, I cannot surmount a deficiency that makes prisoner sometimes of the place, sometimes of the moment where I am, and that, with one blow, prevents me from uniting immediately with the whole of extent as with the whole of duration.

Such is the lesson taught the Proustian being by the "Ways" of Guermantes and of Méséglise. Not only do they teach him that, in whatever manner he decides, his choice will be a split one, therefore an exclusion; but they recall to him also that this exclusion extends itself to all the places of space, save to that one which he has chosen, but in which, by his choice, he has enclosed himself as in a dungeon. To decide to go Swann's Way rather than the Guermantes' Way is to renounce for the possession of the single Way of Swann not simply the way of the Guermantes, but all other Ways of the World. Real space, human space, is not then the simultaneity of all the places of which it admits; it is the mutual exclusion of places, of which nonetheless each exists by itself. Singular space, a sort of empty sprinkling of sites, of which each one would exist "in ignorance of all the others," like an archipelago of islands that no ship could cross.

Each place resembles that place of *Jean Santeuil* represented symbolically by a foxglove blossom the hero sees shooting forth and wants to pick: "Far or near did not exist for it, it was separated from the rest of the earth. . . . Jean wished he could take it with him, even if he rooted it up no matter what would be the consequences, and he would have wished also to carry away this narrow valley, to steal this loneliness, which gave him for the first time the feeling of *this thing that was not another, that was* outside of all the others and could never approach any of them."[61]

Each place, like each moment, is "isolated, enclosed, fixed, and lost, far from all the rest."[62]

Is there, then, no means of regaining lost places like lost moments?

PLACES AND moments lost forever?

One recalls the question asked at the beginning of the Proustian novel, and the famous answer brought immediately afterward, by the episode of the madeleine.

Suddenly, by chance, the coincidence of a certain actual sensation and a certain former sensation determines a raising up of memories. The lost moments are found again. From the depths of the past they awaken, set in motion, cross a long zone of forgetfulness, finally to emerge at the surface: "The thing mounts slowly; I experience the resistance, and perceive the confused murmur of the distances crossed over."[63]

". . . Resisting sweetness of this interposed atmosphere, which has the same extent as our life, and which is the whole poetry of memory."[64]

Thanks to memory, time is consequently not lost, and

if time is not lost, neither is space. Beside time regained, space is regained. Or to speak more precisely, there is a space *finally regained,* a space that is found and discovered thanks to the movement released by memory. Till that moment, in fact, as we have seen, the Proustian world would seem to be singularly destitute of space. What did it present? Here and there some dispersed places, and between them less of a space than an absence of space, something at once closed, interrupted, and insurmountable.

And behold, all at once, a movement is completed in this emptiness. For the first time the mind accompanies an object in its progression. Space is consequently not the endless reiteration of an hiatus, the exclusion of all places by all places, the impossibility of transporting oneself from one locality to another. Space is not negative. It is traversible. The object that crosses it reveals it to the mind.

Examples abound of this metamorphosis of space. How many times, under the pressure of some inner event, does one not see in Proust, as in Baudelaire, the unrolling of a mental extent whose amplitude is measured by the intensity of the feeling that is experienced! In the periodical called *Lilas,* Proust, a schoolboy at the time, describes himself as being situated at the median point of an undulatory circle spreading about him the billow of his emotions: "I am at the center of things," he wrote, "of which each one procures for me sensations and feelings magnificent and melancholy, with which I sport."[65]   This centrality of the affective life, this capacity of receiving such or such a species of sensitive activity in order to develop it afterwards into an immense organization of feeling, is what Proust

will never cease to practice for the rest of his existence.
Intermittence of the heart, unforeseen upheaval of love
or of memory, unexpected revelation of the being of others—
on how many occasions does not Proustian thought transform itself into a sort of sensitive point, from which there
radiates the multitude of desires, of reminiscences, of
anguished suppositions?

> When we love, love is too great to be entirely contained
> within us; it radiates toward the loved person.[66]
> Love is perhaps only the spreading of the eddies that,
> following an emotion, stir up the soul.[67]
> We imagine to ourselves that love has for its object a human
> being who can lie down before us enclosed in a body. Alas! It
> is the extension of this being to all the points of space and of
> time that this being has occupied and will occupy.[68]

And above all, this text, in which, to express the enlarging movement of amorous and jealous thought, Proust finds
an image as apt as it is unexpected: "Briefly, Albertine,
like a stone about which snow has gathered, was only the
generating center of an immense construction, which has as
one of its levels the groundwork of my heart."[69]

In this manner, the enormous development taken by the
personage of Albertine in the volumes that immediately pre-
cede the conclusion, the greater and greater place that she
occupies physically in the book, forms the exact equivalent
of the place taken in the mind and heart of the lover by his
obsession with the loved one. Love is essentially an activity
that diffuses itself, that proliferates, that occupies progres-
sively a greater volume. Like a curl of smoke which creates
through the whole sky its own atmosphere, love dilates,
and in dilating, produces around itself its own space.

But what is true for the phenomenon of love is true for every movement of the heart.

What is memory, for example, except starting from a taste, from a scent, from a clamor of bells, identical to those perceived in the depths of the years, a grand movement of reminiscence, which, like a sky-rocket, opens itself up and unfurls a fan of new memories? Also, it is not only the jealous imagination that, with Proust, occupies space. It is also and especially the mnemonic energy itself. One would say that, shut for a long time in the "closed place" where it found itself confined, some magic resemblance is enough to free this energy from its jail, and permit it to expand itself like the genie coming out of the bottle, with a force all the greater for its having stayed prisoner for so long in this place of extreme constriction. And this movement of expansion goes on in an expanse that now appears to be without break and without obstacle, with nothing inter-rupting the progress of the object that is expanding there. The metamorphosis of space is thus more complete than it seemed at first view. Space has not only become a positive and traversible reality; it has broken into a universal con-tinuity the whole length of which, on all sides, thought unrolls itself, persevering in its onrush and carrying always farther its fringe of foam.

Memory or feeling, a force stretches out in Proustian space. It is accompanied by an incessant murmur of words. Continuous movement, incessant murmur! Notwithstanding all that has been said previously on the essentially discon-tinuous character of the Proustian world, the great critic Curtius was not wrong in claiming that the continuity, on the contrary, was one of its most striking traits: "His work," he wrote in speaking of Proust, "appears to us illimitable, more of a continuity than a form of arrested circuits."[70] —And again: "As long as we follow Proust, we are carried away in the infinite current of mind, which knows neither slackening nor death."[71] Words that perhaps to him who pronounced them would no longer be acceptable today, since in the epoch when he pronounced them, the work of Proust was still not entirely published (it could therefore seem interminable, and the critic could not suspect with what precision Proust had fixed the end of this novel); but words which, nonetheless, in the framework where it is necessary to place them, retain their utmost accuracy. Yes, there is with Proust a continuity that appears at heart the same as discontinuity; a continuity that Curtius identifies with what he calls "the infinite stream of the mind," which is, in fact, rightly without end, inexhaustible, which begins under the form of a pristine billow widening in thought, and which is followed by a series of other concentric circles, immediate impressions, reminiscences, images, ratiocinations of all sorts, prolonged anew, beyond the flux of the words serving to express them. From this point of view, nothing appears—even the sole physical aspect—more similar to a *continuum* than the Proustian Word: functionally uninterrupted in its elocutionary activity, which to continue indefinitely the movement of amplification of thought, like an inundation that, without leaving any part empty, would create everywhere its own space with its overflowing.

vi

BUT THIS space, this continuation that creates itself and expands itself, what is it?

To understand it, there is perhaps nothing better to do than to recall the lines, so beautiful and so charged with meaning, that Proust, at the very end of the episode of the madeleine, has consecrated to the resurrection, in his thought, of the image of Combray: "And as in the game in which the Japanese amuse themselves by soaking in a porcelain bowl of water little pieces of paper, till then indistinct, which, hardly have they plunged in, stretch themselves, give themselves proper contours, color themselves, differentiate themselves, become flowers, houses, personages, consistent and recognizable, the same now as all the flowers of our garden and those of M. Swann's park, and the white waterlilies of the Vivonne, and the good people of the village and their little houses, and the

church, and all of Combray and its surroundings, everything that takes form and solidity, sprang into being,
town and gardens, from my cup of tea."[72]

Marvelous text, in which what rises up in the void of
consciousness, like a world destroyed and suddenly re-
created, is from the first the multicolored multitude of
the real, a crowd of human and floral objects that are
poured out from all parts of the town, the gardens, and the
countryside; but it is still, in its totality, Combray itself,
that is, the place these objects occupy and reoccupy; as if
the place itself, under the obliterating and narrowing
action of forgetfulness, had been contracted into the
smallest possible space, and now, under the inverse of the
restorative and amplifying memory, it opened out anew,
filled up again its former framework, regained its stature.
Creation or re-creation of space, the phenomenon of the
madeleine has thus for its consummation the integral
reconstitution of place. Such is the reason for the contrast
one finds between the two descriptions of Combray,
placed by Proust, the one after the other, at the beginning
of his work; the first being the summary description of
a place that subsisted then in the memory of the hero
only as tiny remains ("Thus it was for a long time when,
awakened at night, I called Combray again to mind, I
brought to life once more only that sort of luminous
patch cut out from the midst of indistinct shadows"[73]);
whereas the second description issues, so to speak,
directly, by way of cause to consequence, of a great
mnemonic movement unloosed by the phenomenon of
the madeleine, and triumphantly presents a place entirely
recovered from oblivion. This is nothing more striking

than the contrast established by Proust between an impotent thought, as Mallarmé says, "to swell again from diverse memories," and the sudden flight taken by this same thought, when a great interior experience restores to it its efficacy. Efficacy that without doubt consists first in the power of retracing itself with the same force and the same freshness as of old, so many different images born of a selfsame past and united again, the ones to the others, like a multicolored cluster of grapes; but that holds also, and even more so, the power of enlarging anew the field of consciousness and of restoring all its amplitude where precisely the cluster of images took place. Thus an extraordinary change is accomplished in the very dimensions of the site that is the framework where the prime action of the novel unrolls. Like the latter, as to what regards duration, part of the temporal unity, the briefest that is, a simple moment of consciousness; but to rediscover finally an immense extent of life, of the same fashion, for what is of space, the Proustian novel takes its point of departure in a place as narrow as possible and comparable to the minuscule volume of a cup of tea; but it is to transform it immediately into a place spacious enough to contain a village, a church, some gardens, an adjoining countryside, that is, a vast space, which, however, had contained, like the maximum in the minimum, an initial space most restricted.

From the first, the novel of Proust begins a double reconquest: a reconquest of lost time and a reconquest of lost space. But it is in this manner so that one would be able to ask oneself on what mounts the immense development that follows. Since the result looked for had been obtainable from the beginning, why continue, why not be

content with this double victory almost instantaneously?
It is perhaps because this victory is more apparent than real,
and because, at base, almost up to the end of Proust's novel,
neither time nor space is really or completely regained.

Of the fallacious character of the victory won by the
mind over duration it takes only a little reflection to render
an account. For what is regained is not time; it is only a
few moments of time. The resuscitative power of the
affective memory does not extend for a great distance into
duration beyond the lived moment that constitutes the
foyer of it. Moments, we know, are closed vases abandoned
along the whole length of existence; and while some among
them might fortuitously be regained by those following,
that by no means implies that the mind should be able to
take possession of others, not, above all, from the assemblage of duration, the length of which these brief entities
in themselves had been in turn laid down; no more, moreover, than one is found capable of dissolving the whole of
it into a continuous block of duration: all these moments
that have precisely for their essence their existing in themselves and not being connected to others. So that the
Proustian resurrections, as numerous as they might be
(and they are, on the contrary, very rare) are never able
to reconstitute time, nor to give to it what perhaps is not
its nature to have, a continuity.

But, once more, it is necessary here to establish
undeniably the rigorous parallelism that exists in Proust
between the dialectic of time and that of space. If the
phenomenon of involuntary memory has for effect the
restitution of lost moments, it restores also lost places. And
in the same way that regained moments keep together

through time, without confounding themselves with it, their little particular durations (similar to the sound of small bells, which continued to support him without discontinuity in the memory of the hero after so many years), the same it is with lost places: forgotten, fragmented, they find themselves to be what they were, reoccupying their proper space. That they might be, moreover, the variations of the image they present, these places do not incorporate themselves either into external space, or into duration. Their continuity is that of their persistence to be, just as it is also that of space, so to speak, *private*, in the interior of which, turn by turn, they shrink and they swell, they remain sealed. Just as the whole of Combray coming forth from a cup of tea reoccupies the extent that was its own, so that extent does not attach itself to the rest of space. In imitation of regained moments, regained places remain isolated entities, between which there is nothing. The miracle of the madeleine has no longer the power to establish a space any more than to establish a duration. It can only make rise up from the depths of the mind the image of closed places, like closed moments.

In a word, when, by the phenomenon of the involuntary memory, the Proustian being retakes possession of his lost moments and places, he has still not resolved his problem. Everything remains still to be done. And there remains in particular the constructing of a space, with the wherewithal to do this only a handful of scattered places, which insist on existing each one on its own "way," at a distance, without the least communication between them.

HOW TO put in communication places that only exist independently of one another?

By local movement, displacement of space.

Of all the movements of this sort, the one found most in evidence in the Proustian universe is travel.

Short trips on foot, walks on the Méséglise Way or along the Vivonne; excursions along the Normandy shore in the carriage of Madame de Villeparisis, or by auto with Albertine; trips on the small local railway to Rivebelle or to Raspelière, with the Verdurins; imaginary journeys to Florence, to Venice; real journeys to Balbec, to Doncières, to Venice again; the whole Proustian work is full of these changes of place. They have a role at least as important as memories. Besides, between the memories and the travels there is an incontestable analogy. The ones and the others are events that break up the inertia of the body and the indolence of the mind. They create a new point of departure in transporting the human being outside the material or spiritual place in which it seemed compelled to live. Above all, travels and memories connect abruptly regions of the earth or of the mind that, heretofore, were without any relation.

There is even in the very experience of the voyage something more marvelous than in the memory; for memory joins only those things that resemble each other. On the contrary, travel makes neighbors of places without any likeness. It links sites that belong to different planes of existence.

One could not insist enough on the surprising and even veritably unheard of kind of travel in the Proustian work. For it breaks a law; it violates a rule that, with Proust, has a sphere of application that is literally universal; and because of this fact, it changes the aspect of the universe. Travel turns upside down the appearance of things. More precisely, it seriously alters the situation in which they exist, the ones in connection with the others. Before it happens, places are like closed vases between which distances set up insurmountable barriers. And behold, these barriers fall, distances are abolished, and to separate places there succeeds a sort of neighborhood. Hence nothing is more disconcerting than the metamorphosis of space brought about by the experience of travel. It is vain to wish to vindicate it, to explain it, to try to eliminate the contradictions it implies. The experience of travel is as inexplicable with Proust as the experience of memory. Unexpected, unprepared for, and explicitly contrary to all antecedent experience, it rises up all at once as a celestial favor to save the human being who experiences it, if not from despair, at least from paralysis. All travel, even without a flying carpet, is for Proust a magical action.

Magical, or, if one wishes, supernatural. In fact there is nothing more like the Proustian voyage than the way in which, to quote the theologians, the angels change places. For Saint Bonaventure or Saint Thomas, an angel, in passing from one place to another, has no need at all of traversing an intermediate space. He is here this instant; he is there the following instant. Distance is not consumed. It is abolished. The angelic being joins at once, and without there having been the slightest gap between them, places the farthest removed.

The Proustian creature does exactly the same thing:

> But finally the specific pleasure of travel is not to descend on the way and to stop when one is tired; it is rather to render the difference between departure and arrival not as imperceptible but as profound as one can make it, to feel it in its totality: intact, such as it was in us when our imagination carried us from the place where we lived into the heart of a place we desired, in a bond that seemed less miraculous because it leaped over a distance, than because it united two separate individualities on this earth. . . .[74]

To put it briefly, the ideal voyage for Proust is the one that, suddenly abolishing distances, places side by side, as if they were contiguous and even communicants, two of those places whose originality, however, was that they seemed to be bound to exist aside from one another, without possibility of communication.

Thus it is fair to say that the experience of movement

changes the laws of the universe. For the first among them, the one that was inscribed at the very beginning of the work, was that there was on the one hand Méséglise and on other Guermantes; and that it was inconceivable that these two Ways could ever be joined. But it suffices, after having walked on foot, to get into a carriage, or to exchange a slow vehicle for a fast one, for the dimensions of time and of space to be changed: "A village that seemed in another world from such another *became its neighbor.*"[75] Méséglise becomes the neighbor of Guermantes. They find themselves close to each other on a common afternoon and in a common world.

Places are then no longer irremedially isolated; they are no longer condemned to be accessible only through one unique Way, itself exclusive of all others. Places hold fast. Their Ways touch. Motion permits their passing from one to another. We are no longer in a universe where incommunicability and distance dominate. One could say that, without losing their own originality, but animated by the social need of drawing together, of forming clusters, of establishing between them relations of good neighborliness, places do their utmost in order to diminish, even indeed, to make disappear, the interval that separates them. And the more striking effect of movement, by which the traveler (imaginary or real) passes from one place to another, is that he seems to transmit to the very places the mobility and the unifying activity that animate him in such a way that places, they also, set in motion and, as if driven by a profound instinct of gregariousness, draw closer to one another.

Of this transmission of movement even to places, the

most famous example is assuredly that of the spires of Martinville. They have often been studied, now and then excellently, as by Du Bos and by Bernard Guyon. But what perhaps the commentators have failed to remark is that primordially this episode expresses a movement of conjunction, and that not only on the part of the traveler towards the landscape, but on the part of the different parts of the landscape towards each other. For the kind of eddy unloosed in the perspective by the constant variations of points of view, because of the windings of the road followed by the carriage (whether it be drawn by the horse of Doctor Percepied, in the novel proper, or the auto driven by the chauffeur Agostinelli, in the version of *Figaro* and of the *Pastiches et Mélanges,* matters little); this kind of eddy has for its immediate and essential consequence, not to bring forth, as in the case of the nocturnal awakening, a vacillating or a whirling of landscape, but, on the contrary, as in a painting by Cézanne, where all the lines and masses take on one meaning, to arrange things in such a way that the various liberated elements hurry up to use their newly acquired mobility in order to bring themselves together and thus to form a new creation.

Nothing is more characteristic of this haste and need for union than the motion described by the third spire, that of Vieuxvicq, situated at first at some distance from the others. Twice, in the two versions of the incident, which follow each other in the text of the novel, the author made a special point, as if to do it honor, to summon aside the spire of Vieuxvicq, to put in relief the bigger effort, and consequently the more meritorious, which it accomplishes in order to draw nearer together with the

other two towers: "At the turning of a road I suddenly
experienced this special pleasure that was not like any
other, the perceiving of the two spires of Martinville, on
which the setting sun shone, and to which the movement
of our carriage and the windings of the road gave the air
of bringing about a changing of place; then the spire of
Vieuxvicq, which, separated from them by a hill and a
valley, and situated on a higher ground in the distance,
seemed nevertheless to be their neighbor."[76]

Now if it becomes their neighbor, that is by a movement whose dynamism is admirably expressed in the
second version: "Alone, rising up from the level of the
plain, and as if lost somewhere in the open country, there
mounted toward the sky the two spires of Martinville.
Soon we saw three of them: coming to place itself in
front of them by a daring volte-face, a late spire, that of
Vieuxvicq, rejoined them."[77]

A junction of sites until then separated, a profound
unification of forms earlier scattered in space, such is the
lesson given us by the three spires: "I saw them," says
Proust, "timidly searching their road and, after some
awkward stumblings of their noble silhouettes, pressing
close against each other, slipping the one behind another,
making now against the still rosy sky only one black
form. . . ."[78]—The final vision of the three spires, given by
Proust, has then for its object one unique form, a perfect,
total form in which are reabsorbed the three antecedent
forms, and a last state of movement by which they have
constantly changed position and even direction. This
changing of direction is especially remarkable. It is as if,
in order to arrive at a terminal unity, there had been

need not only of a movement implicating the whole landscape, but also of a motion of an especial kind, one by which the windings of the route and the turnings of the carriage made ceaselessly change the spires of place, that is, made them occupy different and even opposite points of space. Now it would be possible to see there only the contingent and fortuitous characteristic of the event in question if, in several other essential passages of Proust, the same conditions and the same particular kind of movement were not repeated in order to produce in the end an identical effect.

One may notice them, for example, in the description of a sunrise admired by the main personage when he goes on the train to Balbec. The railroad track being as sinuous as the winding route leading to Martinville (and as the road later followed by the small local railway along the Normandy coast), there results from it a movement of oscillation analogous to that described in the previous case, a perspective ceaselessly turned topsy-turvy, and the opposite points of the landscape seeming at each instant to change places:

> The line of the railroad having changed direction, the
> train turned, the early morning scene was replaced in the frame-
> work of the window by a village of night. . . . I was desolate
> at having lost my band of rosy sky when I perceived it anew,
> but red this time in the window opposite that it abandoned
> to the turning of the railway; so that I spent my time *in running
> from one window to the other in order to bring it near again,
> in order to put on a new canvas the intermittent and opposite
> fragments* of my beautiful morning, scarlet, versatile, and
> *having in it a total view and a continuous painting.*[79]

A passage of importance almost without equal, since it informs us on the final intention of the Proustian movement. It is no longer a question here of binding two objects together; it is a question of bringing them nearer in such a way that both of them, which are opposite, fragmentary, and bounded in time as in extent, form a totality and a continuity. Totality, continuity, which are obtained, a little as in Nicholas of Cusa or Pascal, through the coincidence of contraries. The day and the night, the near and the far, the left and the right, in brief, the eternal Guermantes Way and the eternal Méséglise Way appear here finally as conciliated, unified. And the strangest thing is that this unification is obtained, not by a simplification, but, on the contrary, by a multiplication of the aspects offered by opposed objects; as if it were only in taking consciousness of the inexhaustible variety they present that one could arrive at understanding their true nature, as well as the nature of the relation they maintain with the objects to which they are opposed and form a counterpart.

Thus objects, beings, places lose their exclusiveness without losing their originality. Each thing is in rapport with an infinity of others; each being, like each place, offers an infinity of possible positions, from the one to the other of which one sees them pass. Neither a being, nor an object, nor a place ever finds itself in *One Way,* but in one, in the other, and in all ways. Each being, each thing, each site is similar to this town, of which Proust says, "which while the train follows its *twisting way* appears to us now on our right, now on our left."[80] That was true of the spires of Martinville; it was also true of the sunrise, seen now through one window of the train, now through another; and thus it is, in short, true of all the sites perceived in this essentially sinuous movement, which makes one see the various aspects. It is then that *"the multiple changes of perspective* make a house play at puss in the corner with a hill, a church, and the sea."[81]—In another place Proust writes, "At each *turning* a new part is added."[82] At each turning of the road, at each turning of existence. For it is not only the physical roads that depict curves now and then surprising, and the towers and houses are not the only objects that our movement makes revolve with the land-scape that surrounds them (as a woman would turn herself around to show herself to us in a new dress); often those who know us, or think they know us, become other beings, "as soon as we come up to them from a different side."[83] So Gilberte, so Albertine; so, says Proust, the Guermantes were always "rising up *from one or another of the hazards and sinuosities of my life, like a castle which, on the railroad, one sees again, now on the left, now on the right."*[84]

A double sinuosity thus finally affects space: a sinuosity of aspects presented by the contemplated object; the sinuosity of the road followed by the eye of the mobile spectator (like the look that an unquiet movement of sad curiosity forces ceaselessly to go from one to another point of view, and which Proust calls *"the turning fires of jealousy."*)[85]

That this phenomenon should take place there is no need to be moved oneself, nor to be in a moving vehicle. Thus it suffices to see the sunlight change places on a landscape, in order that the latter modify itself gradually before our eyes, as if we turned ourselves about to see it better: "When in the morning the sun came up from behind the hotel, revealing to me the illuminated beaches as far as the first buttresses of the sea, it seemed to show me another face of them and to engage me in following on the turning route of its rays a voyage motionless and variegated across the most beautiful sites of the landscape broken by the hours."[86]

What will the Proustian novel be, taken in its totality, if not an immense landscape whose turning light makes successively multiple aspects appear? With the result that the sinuous displacement, in constantly changing the lighting, is not a fortuitous characteristic, a negligence of an idiosyncracy of the writer; it is a *method*, in the Cartesian sense of the term; that is, a totality of reasoned proceedings for approximating reality.

AMONG THE rich episodes in change of perspective that abound in *A la recherche du temps perdu*, there is not one more filled with details of all sorts than that in which one sees the hero come close to Albertine's cheek to kiss her.

Although it is long, this scene is so curiously shaded that it is necessary to cite all of it in its completeness:

> Gradually as my mouth began to approach the cheeks that my glances upon them had proposed to embrace, my glances, moving, perceived new cheeks; her neck, seen closer, and as through a magnifying glass, showed in its granulated texture a robustness that modified the character of her face.
>
> The latest applications of photography, which lay down at the feet of a cathedral all the houses that appeared to us so often from close by almost as high as the towers, make successively maneuver, like a regiment, in files, in dispersed order, in serried masses the same monuments; bring nearer, one against the other, the two columns of the Piazetta, present-

ly so distant, move away the near Salute and in a depth pale and defaced succeed in crowding an immense horizon under the arch of a bridge, in the recess of a window, between the leaves of a tree situated on the foreground and of a more vigorous tone; give successively for a framework to the selfsame church the arcades of all the others—I do not see that which might, as much as the kiss, *rise up from what we believed a thing of definite aspect, the hundred other things that it is also as well,* since each is relative to a perspective no less legitimate. In brief, in the same way as at Balbec, Albertine had often appeared to me different now—as if in accelerating prodigiously the rapidity of the *changes in perspective* and of the changes of coloration that a person offers us in our various encounters with her, I had wished to make them all crowd together for some seconds in order to recreate experimentally *the phenomenon that diversifies the individuality of a human being,* and *to draw each from the others as from a box, all the possibilities that it encloses*—in this brief passage of my lips towards her cheek, it was ten Albertines that I saw; this single young girl, looking like a goddess with several heads, this one that I had seen at last, if I tried to approach it, gave place to another.[87]

As singular as that might seem, there is a manifest analogy between the behavior of Albertine's cheeks and the behavior of the towers of Martinville in the text cited above. In one case as in the other, the spectator is witness to an astonishing change of perspective, in which space wholly conspires and which is determined by a movement whose end would be bound to be the junction of elements previously separated. But when, in the case of the spires of Martinville, what was scattered comes closer, and what had been separated is united, it is not at all the same in the episode one has just read. There, the displacement of the constituent elements has not for effect the reducing of the number or the simplifying of the aspects of it. One stupefying multiplicity is revealed here. Far from ending in a check, the experience has as a direct consequence an excess of riches. Nevertheless it is clear that the result of the operation is no longer, as in the other case, a synthesizing of the real, but, on the contrary, a sort of explosion of the latter into a multitude of aspects, each of which equally compels the attention. In a word, "from one thing of definite aspect" there emerge "the hundred other things that it is as well." Under the dominion of a process of renewal, which *on all sides* makes rise up new aspects of a particular being, this one enlarges itself from all the possibles. It is as if, in the same way as it has happened more than once in the history of men, the explorer of space had discovered a fabulously rich world, but not, precisely, the one he wished to discover. Driven by a profound need of unity, wishing at all costs to do away with the isolation in which in his universe all original individualities were surrounded, Marcel Proust had invented a method that could have no other goal than the bringing everywhere of all things together. Now we see that in the very act by which beings are brought together, they are divided in two; they are increased tenfold; they produce a great variety of appearances, from the one to the other of which the mind is ceaselessly thrown back. In the very measure by which beings reveal the inexhaustible diversity of the aspects within them, they escape all observation. The more they reveal themselves, the more completely they disappear. Albertine multiplied tenfold is already Albertine vanished. The true image is lost in the midst of a crowd of masks. Is there even a true image?

Incapable of choosing between so many incarnations, all at the same time so true and so deceitful, the mind finds itself assailed by an unthinkable plurality that it has itself let loose—and, singular irony—let loose following an action that, it hoped, was going to lead it, entirely on the contrary, to unity.

The experience of movement ends, therefore, in a kind of defeat. All along the Proustian novel, despite the frequent movements in which the author, yielding to temptation, has, so to speak, surrendered his text to the invasion of adventitious flora, one feels his suspicion with regard to a proliferation, which he knew was difficult to stop. Better not to mix the Ways, better to avoid the too prolific encounters, better to keep things and beings in their characteristic isolation. Is there still no means of disposing of the "ways" in such a fashion that, without losing their individuality and their independence, they would no longer manifest, the ones against the others, the same exclusiveness, the same aversion? Cannot one place them side by side, in a proximity that would not be an identity? Such is the new solution to his problem, which Proust attempts to put into practice. After the method of *displacement* there remains that of *juxtaposition.*

ix

BUT WHAT is it, to juxtapose?

It is to place one thing *beside* another.

Beside, and not above! In fact it is necessary carefully to distinguish juxtaposition from its analogue, superposition. The one and the other imply the presence of two contiguous, but not blended, realities, located in such a way that the mind goes from one to the other without confounding them and without multiplying them. But justaposition assumes the simultaneity of the two conjoined realities, whereas superposition requires the disappearance of the one so that the appearance of the other may take place.

Proust has hesitated more than once between these two procedures.

That of superposition, is it not the more equitable, that is, the one that reproduces the more adequately the essentially temporal character of existence? "Our Self is made," writes Proust, *"from the superposition of our successive states."*[88] What is true of ourselves is still truer of the image, or rather the series of images presented by the human beings we know. Thus, the main personage of the Proustian novel speaks somewhere of *"the superposition of the successive images* that Albertine had been for him";[89] an experience that, for him, had already happened in his dealings with the Duchess of Guermantes, in which he had seen "so many different women *superimpose themselves, each one disappearing when the following one had taken on enough body."*[90]

To superimpose the successive images of human beings, therefore, is to act like the reality of time does; it is to hide away what no longer is, in order to make place for what is coming to be. Superposition is the act by which, in establishing oneself, in occupying the whole surface, in making disappear under its mass the anterior images, the actual moment consummates its victory over the past; and, at the same time, the act by which, in letting itself be buried, the past acknowledges its defeat. Every work that tries to reproduce this double movement of invading and burying uses one form or another of superimposition. Each new page ends by *hiding* the preceding page. One thinks of certain poems from Keats to Pater, of the *Nourritures terrestres,* of the novels of Virginia Woolf; one thinks of the Bergsonian philosophy.

One must acknowledge that there is nothing that less resembles the Proustian experience of the real.

The experience of Proust is not at all the burial of the past under the present; quite the contrary, it is a resurrection of the past in spite of the present. Proust dreams of a kind of superposition periodically or irregularly broken by an inverse phenomenon of upheaval. He conceives of a superposition of a geological and Plutonian type, a sort of unstable stratification, where, from time to time, "the upheavals bring to the level of the surface old strata."[91] Or he imagines an arrangement similar to that of the magic lantern. Of course, as to what concerns its internal functioning, the magic lantern offers a process that one should not confound with superposition. It does not conceal; it supersedes. To the previous moment, through a mixed movement, interrupted and abrupt, which, besides, is bound to please Proust more than the fluid and uninterrupted gliding of cinematographic images, it substitutes a subsequent moment that involves the total annihilation of the one preceding it. The Proustian universe is not, therefore, that of the magic lantern; or, if one wishes, it is just that, but on the condition of imagining the painted plates not in the motion that projects the ones *after* the others, but arranged, the ones *beside* the others, in a simultaneous order. In short, the glass plates of the lantern offer a collection of *stained glass windows,* as in the church at Combray.

But the stained glass windows are juxtaposed; they are neither superimposed, nor substituted.

It is true that, seen from a certain angle, the phenomenon of the magic lantern offers the example, unexpected, staggering, and nevertheless profoundly fascinating, of a *superposition juxtaposed.* In projecting an image on a wall, the lantern covers the wall but does not disguise it; so well that the image and the wall appear simultaneously, the one under the other. The body of Golo does not hide the doorknob. In the same way, would it not be possible to imagine a world in which the ordinary opacity of beings, of places, of moments, would have given place to a certain transparency, so that in plunging his gaze into the depths of his own being, one could see the various epochs of it rise tier upon tier like the cells in a beehive? Is not there somehow the final vision that those trembling giants have of themselves in *Temps retrouvé*, perched by Proust on the heights made of the succesive and semitransparent layers of duration? Whatever is the case, the theme of the magic lantern, placed by Proust at the beginning of his work, like that of the puppets placed by Goethe at the beginning of his *Wilhelm Meister*, has, it seems, a definite mission, that of expressing a paradox on which the Proustian novel will rest: the simultaneity of the successive, the presence, in the present, of *another* present: the past.

The Proustian novel is often this: a series of images that, from the depths where they have been buried, rise to the light of day. A struggle for life bursts out between them and those that occupied the surface. There sometimes results from it a vertigo, this vacillation of places and of times, of which we spoke at the beginning.

But we know that the Proustian work does not seek to shut itself up in that confused zone where entangled images are brought face to face. It is a question, on the contrary, of arriving at the maximum of clearness. Now that is possible only if, giving up the idea of a vertical representation of the real, our thought distributes the different elements of the real on a horizontal plane; that is, on a surface where, the ones situated beside and not above the others, they present themselves isolated, distinct, and nonetheless simultaneously to the gaze.

Such is the operation of juxtaposition. One finds it employed everywhere in Proust, as well as to represent the images of dream and of memory as those of present reality:

> It was the season when the Bois de Boulogne reveals the most various essences and juxtaposes the greatest number of distinct parts of a composite collection.[92]
>
> When in revery we reflect, in order to return to the past, we try to slow down, to suspend the perpetual movement in which we are swept along, little by little we see reappear, juxtaposed but entirely distinct the ones from the others, the shades which in the course of our existence a single name presented to us successively.[93]

To be brief, juxtaposition is the contrary of motion. It is an assemblage of objects that remain in their place, in fixed premises, while the movement just mentioned is a displacement that transfers an image of the past into the present, or that makes the different parts of a landscape "play at puss in the corner." In the juxtaposition, no distance is leaped over; no overturning of the situation is accomplished; no unification or multiplication is realized. Very simply, things that exist are happy to continue their existence, the ones nearby the others, without drawing closer to each other or thrusting away each other. They get aligned, each by the side of the others, as if they were in the same showcase.

Now such is precisely the metaphor of which Proust avails himself to represent this static situation: "In the name of Balbec," he writes, "as in the magnifying glass of one of these penholders one buys at seaside resorts, I perceived waves upheaving about a church of Persian style."[94] If the gaze is aided here by a sort of magnifying glass, it is not to enlarge the objects, it is rather to isolate them, to put them in relief, and thus to reveal much more sharply how surprising is their conjugated presence. In the name of Balbec there can be noticed, coupled, two unassimilable elements, a Normandy shore and the Persian style of a church. No effort is made to unite their disparate traits. Our thought contents itself in perceiving them together, and in arranging them in one composite whole.

An example of exceptional value of this *composition by juxtaposition* is given us by another name of a city, that of Florence:

> One year when my father had decided that we would go to spend the Easter vacation at Florence and at Venice, not having yet the chance to comprise in the name of Florence the elements that usually compose cities, I was constrained to conjure forth a supernatural city of the impregnation, by certain springlike perfumes, of what I believed to be in its essence, the genius of Giotto. At the utmost—and because one cannot make hold in a name very much more of duration than of space—like certain paintings of Giotto themselves, which show at two different moments of action the same character, here lying on his bed, there preparing to mount a horse, the name of Florence was divided into two compartments. In the one, under an architectural canopy, I contemplated a fresco . . . ; in the other . . . I traversed rapidly the Ponte Vecchio, crowded with daffodils, narcissus, and anemones.[95]

Few passages show us with as much clarity the process of transformation that Proust imposes on images. In the name there is enclosed a place; in the place there is enclosed a being; finally from the place, so named and animated, revealing itself to have, like the Balbec of the text previously cited, two principal attributes—namely, its springlike and

flowery aspect, and its reputation as the city of art—there
follows that the dreamer imagines himself at the center of
two scenes, where he sees himself first in the course of
contemplating frescoes, and, second, in the midst of flowers.
These two scenes necessarily evoke successive aspects of
the sojourn supposedly made by the dreamer in Florence;
but what is essential to remark is that, resuming this
sojourn in "two different moments of action," which
mean to express the beauties and the delights of it all, the
dreamer depicts them in a way that itself, is not at all
successive, since it consists in the arranging, one beside the
other, of two pictures of equal importance in such manner
that the order in which they are presented could be re-
versed. Hence, how is one not to think here of these
pictures, or still more, of those frescoes of Giotto to
which the author refers himself, in which the painter
applied himself to the task of retracing a series of episodes
in the life of a certain holy personage in such a manner
that the latter, in place of being narrated, as by a hagi-
ographer of a *Légende dorée* in the continuity of its
duration, is simply exhibited in a small number of exem-
plary scenes reflecting the diversity of adventures or the
number of virtues of him who is to be considered? Instead
of a curve of existence, a sequence composed of isolated
scenes, of which each one has its own significance, and
which have for their only common trait their relationship
to the same person whose noble exploits, well-compartmented,
have the air of being placed there, the ones beside the
others, in a purely simultaneous order. No doubt, in the
case of Giotto, we find ourselves in the presence of a
series of pictures, whereas in that of the revery provoked by

the name of Florence, the inventive thought of the Proustian personage does not go beyond a double panel. But it is not without interest to catch the Proustian imagination in its beginning, at the moment at which it is still content to introduce a minimum of plurality in its reconstruction of the events of real life or of dream. Later, augmenting the number of scenes that it depicts, it will metamorphose itself into an edifice covered with frescoes and into a gallery full of pictures.

Essential form of creative thought with Proust, and what one can still distinguish in a letter from Proust to Reynaldo Hahn,[96] accompanied by a sketch representing a double scene inscribed in the two parts of a stained glass window. As can be seen, nothing is more spontaneous in the world than, for representing what it invents or recalls, the way Proustian thought adopts the form of an assemblage of two or several more pictures. From this point of view, the central personage of *A la recherche du temps perdu* behaves exactly like Proust himself. Learning that the present Duke of Wurtemberg's mother was a daughter of Louis-Philippe, he immediately contemplates in his mind "a whole reliquary, similar to those painted by Carpaccio or Memmling,"[97] in which, in an early picture, the princess appears at the wedding of one of her brothers; whereas in the final episode she is in bed, giving birth to a boy.

The resemblance to the texts cited above is striking. Without any doubt, we have there a specifically Proustian trait, such a one that it would be difficult to find its equivalent with any great modern novelist. The more often, in fact, the latter does not seek to depend on scenes; it is human existence in its gradual development that means something to him, that is, the sort of thing that does not appear *in* pictures, but only *between* them; whereas Proust is less fascinated by the continuity of an action than by the instantaneity of an attitude, of an expression, of a simple "stage play" of whom no one better than he, by the way, understands the implication. One is to recollect the "voyeur" side of the Proustian personage, the pleasure he experiences in surprising people, in spying upon certain spectacles. Nothing pleases him like perceiving in the framework of a lighted window, such as it was on his night walks in Doncieres, such "veridical and mysterious scenes of life," into which, he says, "I did not penetrate."[98] Observed thus, from the outside, at intervals, by a series of glances that cut it out, the world divides itself into compartments, in the interior of each of which there is *placed* a different scene. Of this disposition into the form of checker-work, a remarkable example is found in *Le côté du Guermantes*. There, the hero, watching for the return of the duke and duchess, stations himself at the very top of the house, in a room from which one can see the fronts of the opposite houses: "Thus each courtyard," says Proust, "made for the witness next door, through suppressing the noise by its interval, through letting see the silent gestures in a rectangle placed under glass by the closed windows, *an exhibition of a hundred Dutch pictures juxtaposed.*" Juxtaposed! Is not there, realized in an extreme example, the preeminent Proustian method? That which consists in eliminating duration, in suppressing distance, in reducing the world to a number of isolated, contiguous images, strictly delimited, which, hitched, so to

speak, to the same dado-rail, offer themselves simultaneously to the gaze? What is discerned in front of him under the
form of a juxtaposition of scenes is not simply some odd
corners of the universe watched from the top of the House
of Guermantes by the contemplator; it is the entire
Proustian world, such as it appears to the gaze when the
gaze has found its most satisfying point of view. The
hundred Dutch pictures perceived in the framework that
gives out upon the House of Guermantes are a figuration
of the hundred other pictures juxtaposed, which, when
the reader comes, he also, to hoist himself up to a certain
point of view, are disclosed to him there, not less simultaneously disposed, in the whole of the Proustian novel.
And the symbolic character of this vision finds itself con-
siderably reinforced in the lines that follow, by two new
series of images, which, like the preceding ones, have for
their express goal to let us comprehend better what a
Proustian universe is, a universe where everything is juxtaposed. It is firstly a house lighted from top to bottom,
where the activity of the inhabitants is perceived at all
stages; the other is the image of a hill road of which one
distinguishes all its windings: "When the large square
windows (of the House of Silistrie, which were opposite),
dazzled by the sun like sheets of rock crystal, were
opened for the household, one had to follow at different
stages the footmen, impossible to distinguish clearly,
but who beat the carpets, the same pleasure as to see in a
landscape by Turner or Elstir, a traveler in a stagecoach,
or a guide at different degrees of altitude on the Saint-
Gothard."[99]

At this point, the Proustian imagination results in a

vision that comes close to that of Piranesi: a figure appears there in profile, in a repeated manner, that of a human being always recognizable, but each time in different conditions, and enclosed each time in a strictly limited subdivision of reality. So it is that this face, resembling itself in whatever situation it finds itself, can be identified, it may be, in the Proustian novel, with the central consciousness in which everything is reflected; it may be again, with the genius of the author, his omnipresent activity, which, as varied as the episodes of the novel may be, is made to be recognized there, isolatedly and serially, as their principal unifier. The Proustian juxtaposition is therefore not a simple collection of "views" or of heterogeneous "scenes" such as one finds so often under the form of a plurality of disparate pictures on the walls of certain museums. It is, on the contrary, a multiplicity unified by the active presence of one single actor and one single author.

Perhaps of this relation between the multiplicity and the unity of the work, the symbol that is the clearest, the most explicit, the most deliberately metaphorical of all is that of the bedroom of Marcel at Balbec, a room whose walls are covered over by the glass panels of a library, in the mirrors of which the shades of the sky are reflected in a series of pictures that are all different:

> At the moment when I entered the room, the violet
> sky . . . inclined toward the sea on the hinge of the horizon
> like a religious picture above the high altar, whereas the
> different parts of the sunset, shown in the glass of the lower
> mahogany bookcases, which ran the length of the walls and
> which I related by the thought to the marvelous painting
> from which they were detached, seemed like those different

scenes that some old master had executed long ago for a hunting party, and which one exhibits the ones beside the others, in the room of a museum, on separate panels that only the imagination of the visitor puts in their right place on the predellas of the reredos.[100]

Here the Proustian imagination has finally found the perfect metaphor, that in which the work is represented by means of the most adequate symbolic form. For the panes of glass of the lower bookshelves at Balbec do not reflect only the "different parts" of the sunset; they reproduce again and frame figuratively the various parts of the entire novel. Yes, the work of Proust is made, it also, of a series of detached scenes cut from the course of reality, in such a fashion that almost nothing subsists of the current of reality that passed there. As a set-off, "exhibited the ones beside the others," they are disposed over the length of a surface over which what was temporal is now spread out. Thus time gives place to space. The surface of the novel is occupied by a series of predellas, and that in such a manner that despite the cutting out, the gaps and the limits outlined by the frames, the imagination immediately seizes the principle that unites the predellas and reconstitutes the totality of which they are only sections.

The metaphor is one of absolute appropriateness. It is, besides, only the development of earlier comparisons. The image of the predellas is already in germ in the vision of Florence imagined after the frescoes of Giotto; it is found again in the sequence of imaginary pictures relative to the life of a great lady, conceived under the form of a "reliquary similar to those which Carpaccio or Memmling painted." But it is at the very end of his work that Proust gave to this symbol its most complete development. Recapitulating the number of persons he encountered in the course of his existence, their variety, the intercrossings of the threads that ended by binding them together, the central personage of the novel writes this: "My life was already long enough for more than one of the beings it offered me. I discovered to complete it, another being. As to Elstir's work even, which I saw here, in a place which was the sign of his glory, I was able to add the oldest memories of the Verdurins, the Cottards, the conversation in the restaurant at Rivebelle, the morning I discovered Albertine, and so many others."

And having thus *added* to the actual figure of Elstir older versions and a whole series of witnesses at the same time incomplete and convergent, the author pursues in the following terms, in which there is found, enriched with an essential difference, the theme of the predella and the reredos: "Thus an amateur of art to whom one shows the shutter of a reredos recollects in what particular collection others are dispersed . . . he can reconstitute in his head the predella, the entire altar." [101]

What is here ' the entire altar" that Proust has seen unless it be the work that he writes in its totality? Words of capital importance, since they bring to the work in question at the same time its conclusion and its definition. At the moment the Proustian novel is ended, when the consciousness, which has not ceased to register within all the happenings, is found at the point of throwing upon them a final retrospective and elucidating gaze, then the discontinuous multiplicity of episodes, identical until this moment to a series of isolated and juxtaposed pictures, is found to make room in the mind of him who embraces everything within it, for a coherent reality of images that relate themselves the ones to the others, are mutually lighted up, and, so to speak, *compose themselves.*

One cannot, then, conclude otherwise than in declaring that the Proustian novel *ends* by demonstrating its internal coherence. It reveals it, however, only at the latest possible moment, for it must remain invisible until the moment when the retrospective gaze is found finally in possession of the network of interwoven references, necessary for understanding what has taken place. There is a final moment when what appears is no longer an assemblage of disparate episodes, but an altogetherness, in which above the isolated predellas, a reliquary is discerned, or a reredos. Not that the different panels which compose the entire work are entangled, are grounded together, suppress the intervals which separate them, transform their discontinuity into a tardy continuity. There is not and there cannot be temporal continuity in a work that has for its principles of construction intermittence and occlusion. The Proustian work is made of, and remains made of, distinct episodes. However these episodes are placed in harmony; they exchange information; they confer upon themselves a sort of reciprocal intelligibility. It is as if, instead of succeeding themselves, to each other, they content themselves by simply adding themselves to the whole, in the manner of a series of pictures with which an amateur constantly would enlarge his collection. Thus everything finally depends on a memory that is not the involuntary memory: memory of the total work, memory total in itself, which conserves and reproduces the mass of episodes, as if they had never been a part of time, had never been menaced by forgetfulness. Intact, always similar to themselves, always enclosed, and as if localized in the interior of their frameworks, the episodes of the Proustian novel present themselves in an order which is not temporal, since it is anachronistic, but which cannot be other than spatial, since, like an array of jars of jam in the cupboards of our childhood, it arranges a series of closed vases in the caverns of the mind.

In a word, at the moment when it ends, and where, retrospectively, it reveals itself in its wholeness, Proust's novel has ceased to be temporal; exactly like a history of France *in images,* it is no longer a history; it is a collection of images, which, brought together, furnishes a place and forms *an illustrated space.*

Do not let us be deceived then by the declaration so often reported of Proust, according to which, in his novel, he had wanted to render palpable a fourth dimension, the dimension of time.[102] For the dimension of time is, in his mind, only a dimension entirely similar to all three others, a dimension, itself also, purely spatial. *"Time for him is like space,"* he writes of one of his characters, Jean Santeuil.[103] And in the same way, one can say of his novel what he himself said of a certain place called Guermantes, which like the church of Combray, was full of memories: *"Time has taken there the form of space."*[104]

Now if Proustian time *always* takes the form of space, it is because it is of a nature that is directly opposed to Bergsonian time. Nothing resembles less the melodic continuity of pure duration; but nothing, in return, more resembles what Bergson denounced as being a false duration, a duration the elements of which would be exteriorized, the ones relatively to the others, and aligned, the ones beside the others. Proustian time is time spatialized, juxtaposed. . . .

It could not happen differently, from the moment when Proust had conceived the temporality of his universe under the form of a series of pictures, which, successively presented in the course of the work, would finally reappear all together, simultaneously, to be sure, outside of time, but not outside of space. Proustian space is this final space, made of the order in which there are distributed, the ones in harmony with the others, the different episodes of the Proustian novel. The order is not different from that which binds between them the predellas, and the predellas to the reredos. A plurality of episodes makes way for and constructs its own space, which is the space of the work of art.

notes

1. *Du côté de chez Swann,* vol. I, p. 5. All references are to the
   Pléiade edition.
2. *Contre Sainte-Beuve,* p. 56.
3. Ibid., p. 68.
4. *Du côté de chez Swann,* vol. I, p. 9.
5. *A l'ombre des jeunes filles en fleur,* vol. I, p. 500.
6. Ibid., p. 717.
7. *Le temps retrouvé,* vol. III, pp. 874–875.
8. Ibid.
9. *Du côté de chez Swann,* vol. I, p. 6.
10. Ibid., p. 184.
11. *A l'ombre des jeunes filles en fleur,* vol. I, p. 667.
12. *Du côté de chez Swann,* vol. I, p. 115.
13. *La prisonnière,* vol. III, p. 249.
14. *Du côté de chez Swann,* vol. I, p. 46.
15. Cf. Fernand Gregh, "Mystères," *Revue Blanche,* 15 September
    1896; and René de Messières, "Un document sur Proust,"
    Romanic Review, April 1942. The essential passage in Gregh,

relative to the theme of localization, is the following: "When I am not able to make, as the psychologists say, this *localization*, when to the mystery of memory there is added that of the unconscious, I am vanquished by too much of the inexplicable, I have a dazzlement as if before a prohibited revelation." One knows that the experience of the affective memory, described in these pages by Gregh and attributed in the text to a certain friend V., is very likely the very experience of Proust, as shown by M. de Messières.

16. *Sodome et Gomorrhe,* vol. II, pp. 1028–1029.
17. Ibid.
18. *Pastiches et Mélanges,* p. 249.
19. Ibid.
20. *Du côté de chez Swann,* vol. I, p. 218.
21. *Jean Santeuil,* vol. I, pp. 194–195.
22. *Du côté de chez Swann,* vol. I, p. 171.
23. *Le côté de Guermantes,* vol. II, p. 38.
24. *Sodome et Gomorrhe,* vol. II, p. 943.
25. *Du côté de chez Swann,* vol. I, p. 100. See also *Du côté de chez Swann,* vol. I, pp. 90 and 537.
26. *A l'ombre des jeunes filles en fleur,* vol. I, p. 729. The sentence continues in the following way: "as in certain portraits in which some painters pretend without cheating anyone as to the most exact observation of actual life, but in choosing for their model an *appropriate framework* polo ground, golf course, race track, yacht course, to give a modern equivalent of those canvasses in which the early masters *made the human face appear in the foreground of a landscape."*
27. *A l'ombre des jeunes filles en fleur,* vol. I, p. 833.
28. *La prisonnière,* vol. III, p. 67.
29. Ibid., p. 193.
30. *Le temps retrouvé,* vol. III, p. 989.
31. *A Louisa de Mornand,* Correspondence, vol. V, p. 149.
32. *Contre Sainte-Beuve,* p. 84.
33. *Du côté de chez Swann,* vol. I, p. 156.
34. Ibid., p. 87.

35. *Le côté de Guermantes*, vol. II, p. 204.

36. Ibid., p. 257.

37. *Contre Sainte-Beuve*, p. 274.

38. *Jean Santeuil*, vol. II, p. 336.

39. *Du côté de chez Swann*, vol. I, pp. 387–388.

40. Ibid., p. 116.

41. Ibid., p. 185.

42. Ibid.

43. *Jean Santeuil*, vol. II, p. 317.

44. *A l'ombre des jeunes filles en fleur*, vol. I, p. 676: "The Bay of Balbec was a *small universe apart* in the midst of the great one, a flowerbasket of seasons where there were gathered together in a circle the various days and the successive months."

45. Ibid., p. 721.

46. *Du côté de chez Swann*, vol. I, p. 43.

47. *Les plaisirs et les jours*, p. 216.

48. *La fugitive*, vol. III, p. 529.

49. *La prisonnière*, vol. III, p. 377.

50. Ibid., p. 376.

51. *Du côté de chez Swann*, vol. I, p. 529.

52. Ibid., p. 30.

53. Ibid., p. 13. Marcel longs for the kiss of his mother "for a communion of peace in which my lips would imbibe her *real presence* and the privilege of falling asleep." The expression "real presence" will be found also in the passage cited hereafter.

54. *Le côté de Guermantes*, vol. II, p. 134.

55. *Sodome et Gomorrhe*, vol. II, p. 733.

56. *Jean Santeuil*, vol. I, pp. 80–81.

57. *Les plaisirs et les jours*, p. 47.

58. *Le temps retrouvé*, vol. III, p. 870.

59. Correspondence.

60. *Du côté de chez Swann*, vol. I, p. 135.

61. *Jean Santeuil*, vol. II, p. 43.

62. *Le côté de Guermantes*, vol. II, p. 397.

63. *Du côté de chez Swann*, vol. I, p. 46.

64. *Pastiches et Mélanges*, p. 108.

65. Cf. Robert Dreyfuss, "Marcel Proust au lycée Condorcet," *Revue de France*, December 1925, p. 659.

66. *A l'ombre des jeunes filles en fleur*, vol. I, p. 609.

67. *La prisonnière*, vol. III, p. 20.

68. Ibid., p. 100.

69. *La fugitive*, vol. III, p. 438.

70. Curtius, *Marcel Proust*, ed. of *La Revue nouvelle*, 1928, p. 125.

71. Ibid.

72. *Du côté de chez Swann*, vol. I, pp. 47–48.

73. Ibid., p. 43.

74. *A l'ombre des jeunes filles en fleur*, vol. I, p. 644.

75. *Sodome et Gomorrhe*, vol. II, p. 996.

76. *Du côté de chez Swann*, vol. I, p. 180.

77. Ibid., p. 181.

78. Ibid., p. 182.

79. *A l'ombre des jeunes filles en fleur*, vol. I, p. 874.

80. "Interview Elie-Joseph Blois," *Le Temps*, 12 November 1913.

81. *Sodome et Gomorrhe*, vol. II, p. 1005.

82. Ibid., p. 897.

83. *A l'ombre des jeunes filles en fleur*, vol. I, p. 874.

84. *Contre Sainte-Beuve*, p. 268.

85. *La prisonnière*, vol. III, p. 103.

86. *A l'ombre des jeunes filles en fleur*, vol. I, p. 673.

87. *Le côté de Guermantes*, vol. II, pp. 364–365. One must not omit reading the commentary on this passage in the admirable article by Gérard Benette: "Proust palimseste," *Tel Quel*, Winter 1963, no. 12, pp. 64ff.

88. *La fugitive*, vol. III, p. 544.

89. *La prisonnière*, vol. III, p. 69.

90. *Le côté de Guermantes*, vol. II, p. 531.

91. *La fugitive*, vol. III, p. 544.

92. *Du côté de chez Swann*, vol. I, p. 423.

93. *Le côté de Guermantes*, vol. II, pp. 11–12.

94. *Du côté de chez Swann*, vol. I, p. 389.

95. Ibid., p. 390. See also the article in *Figaro, Vacances de Pâques*, 25 March 1913 *(Chroniques*, p. 108), where, instead of the

name of Giotto, one finds that of Ghirlandaio.

96. *Lettres à Reynaldo Hahn,* ed. Philippe Kolb, NRF, p. 74.
97. *Le côté de Guermantes,* vol. II, p. 536.
98. Ibid., p. 97.
99. Ibid., p. 503.
100. *A l'ombre des jeunes filles en fleur,* vol. I, p. 803.
101. *Le temps retrouvé,* vol. III, p. 973.
102. Ibid., vol. II, p. 256. See also vol. I, p. 186; vol. III, p. 929, 1031 and 1047.
103. *Jean Santeuil,* vol. III, p. 126.
104. *Contre Sainte-Beuve,* p. 285. The spatialization of time in Proust has been luminously demonstrated by Ramón Fernandez *(Messages,* p. 160): "Proust gives to time the value of characters in space, in affirming that the different parts of time reciprocally exclude themselves and remain exterior the ones from the others . . ." See also Joseph Frank, "Spatial Form in Modern Literature," *Sewanee Review,* 1945, p. 249: "By the discontinuous presentation of character, Proust forces the reader to juxtapose disparate images of his characters spatially."

Library of Congress Cataloging in Publication Data

Poulet, Georges.
    Proustian space.

    Translation of L'espace proustien.
    Includes bibliographical references.
        1. Proust, Marcel, 1871–1922—Criticism and
interpretation. I. Title.
PQ2631.R63Z82713   843'.9'12   76–47390
ISBN 0–8018–1921–0

DATE DUE

DEMCO 38-297